COSTUME DESIGN WORKBOOK

TABLE OF CONTENTS

DATE	TITLE	PAGE #

TABLE OF CONTENTS

DATE	TITLE	PAGE #

TABLE OF CONTENTS

DATE	TITLE	PAGE #

TABLE OF CONTENTS

DATE	TITLE	PAGE #

NOTES

NOTES

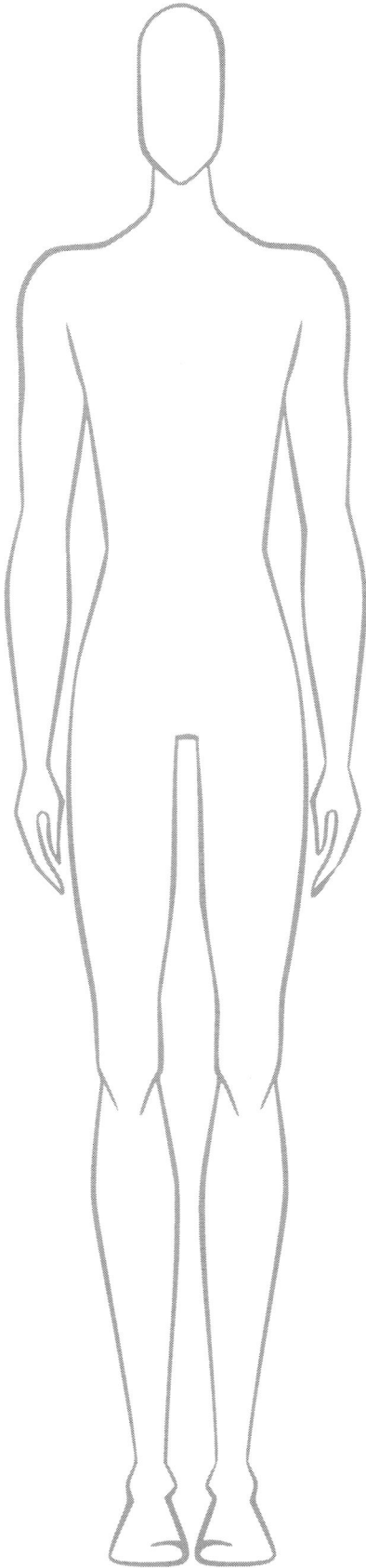

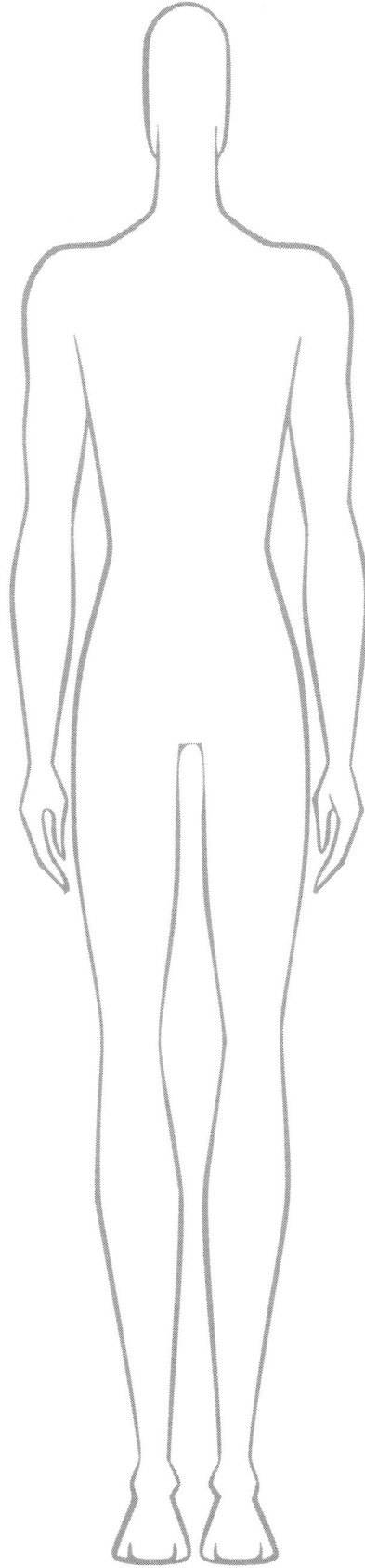

NOTES

NOTES

NOTES

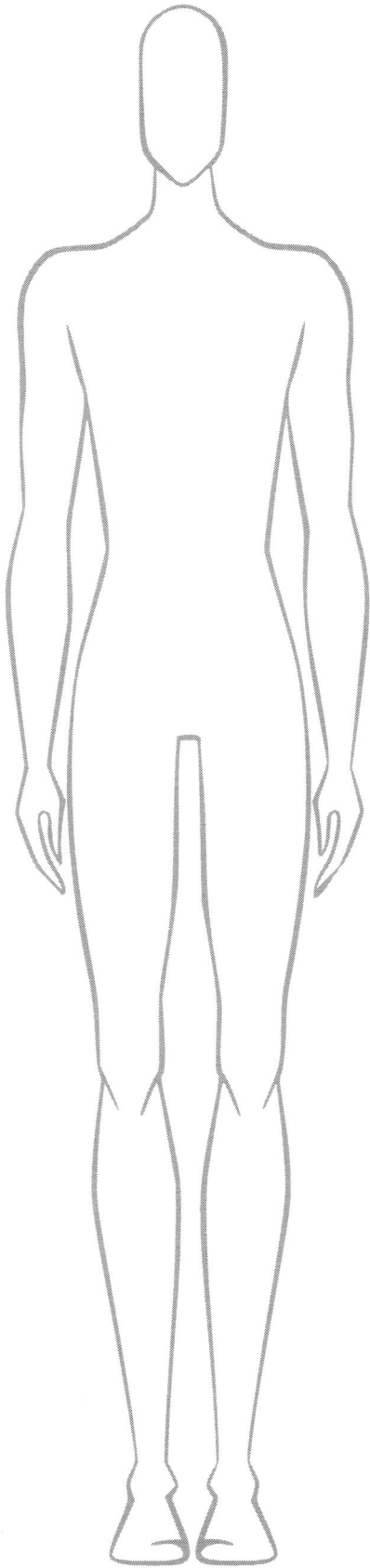

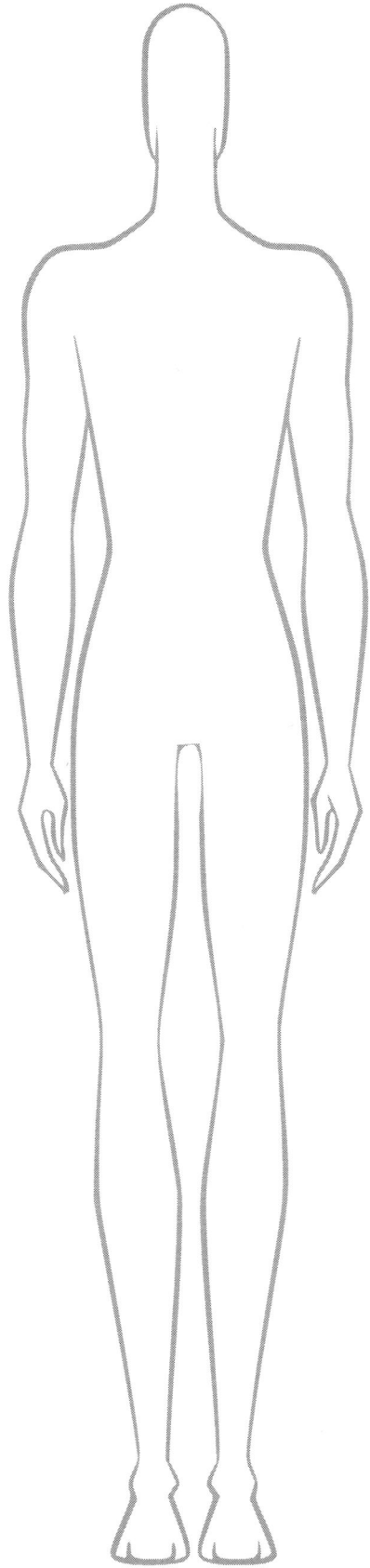

NOTES

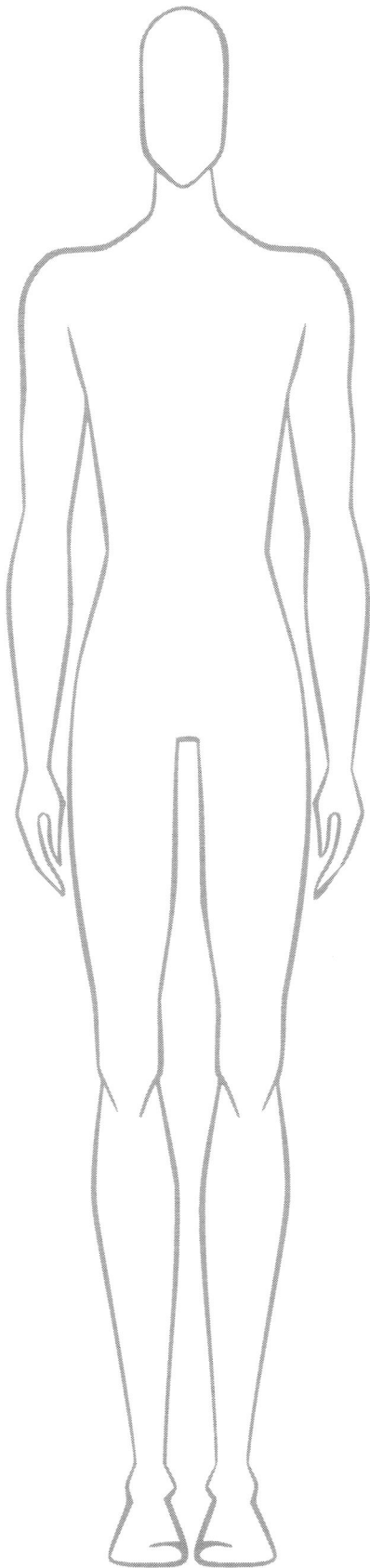

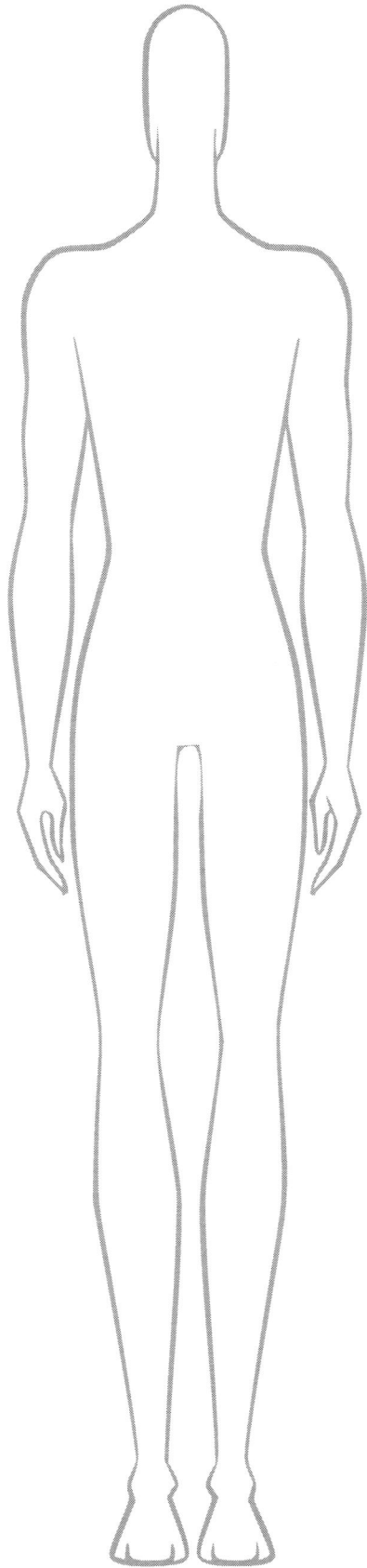

NOTES

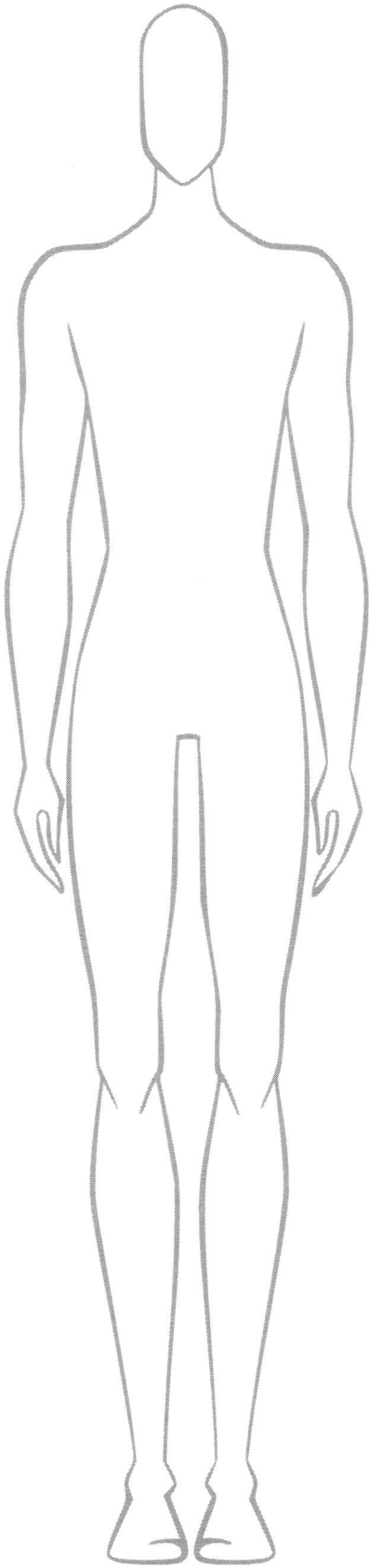

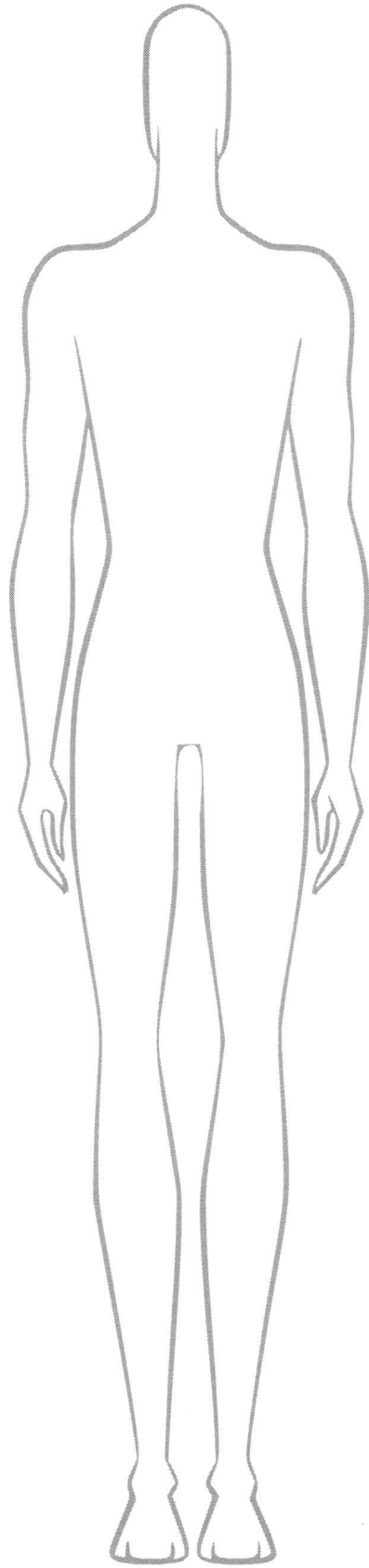

NOTES

NOTES

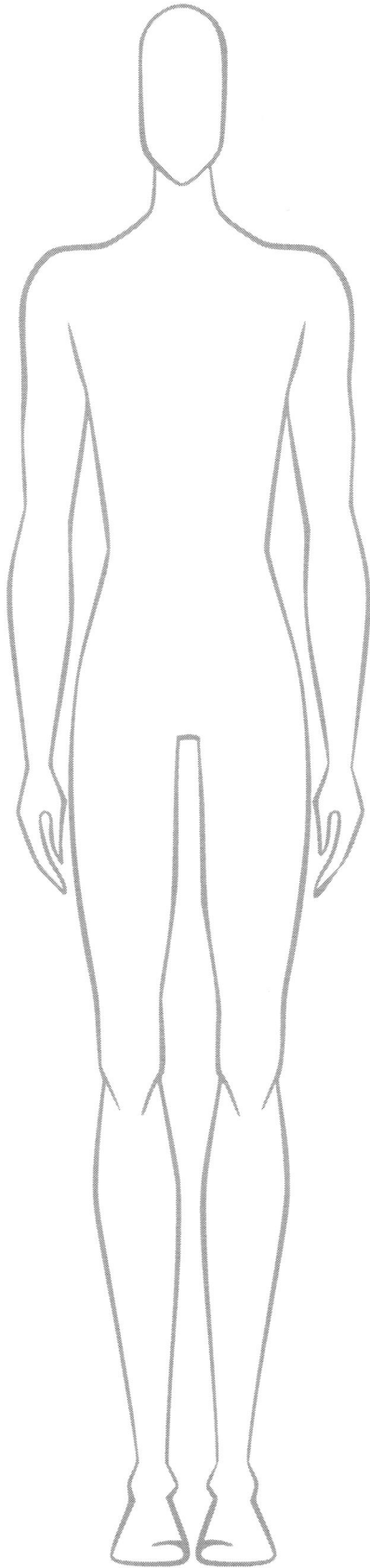

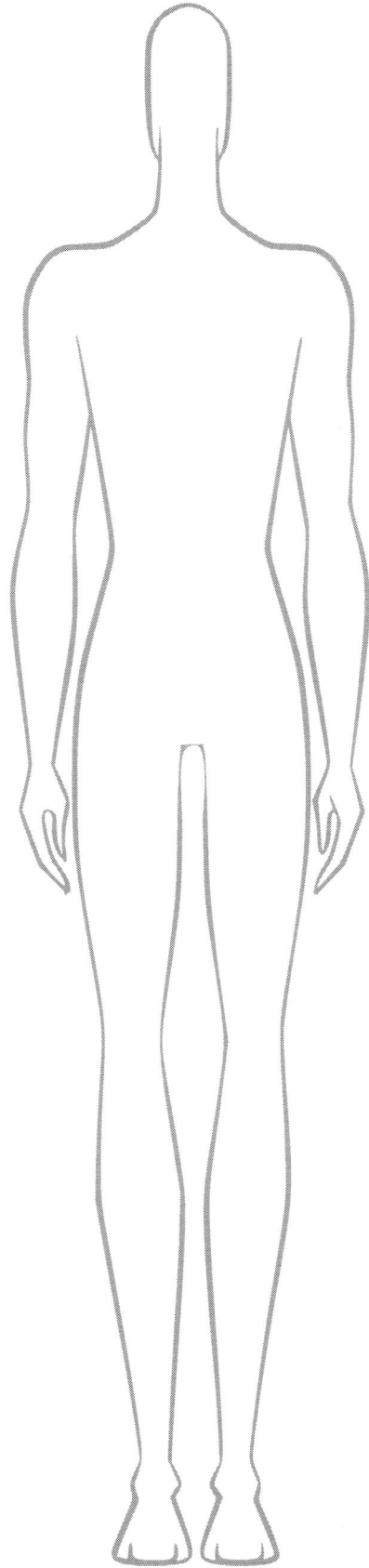

NOTES

NOTES

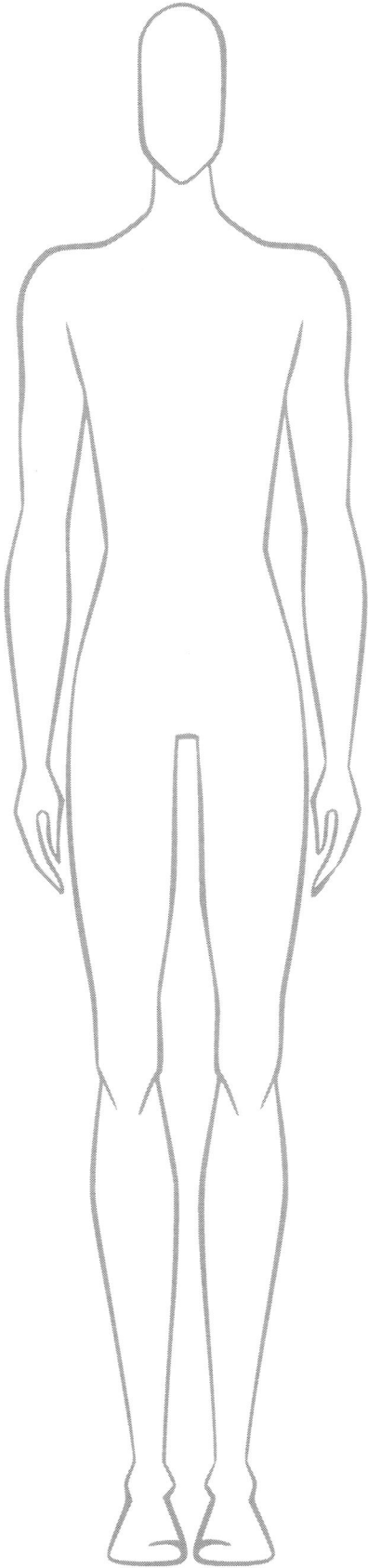

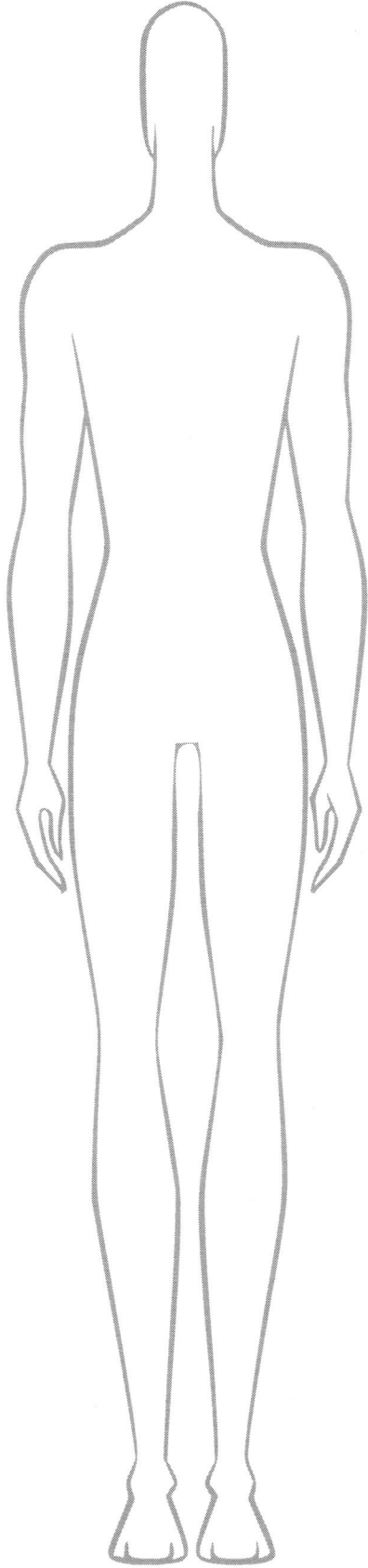

NOTES

NOTES

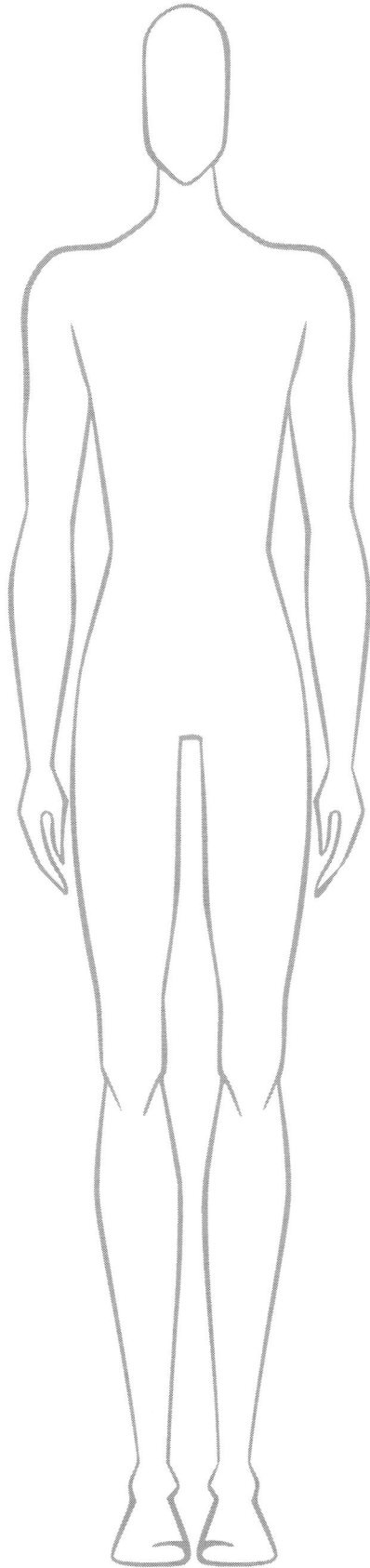

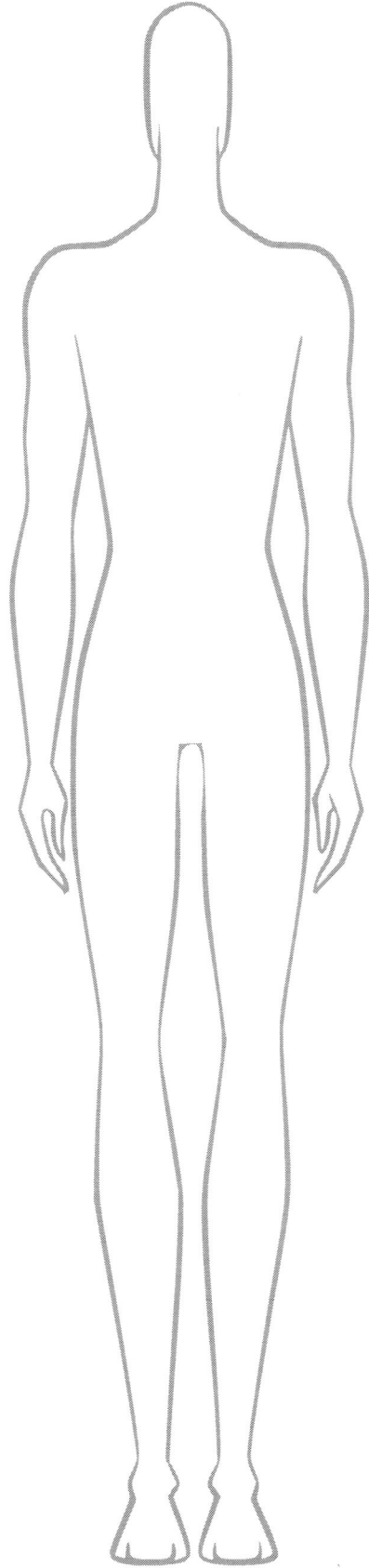

NOTES

NOTES

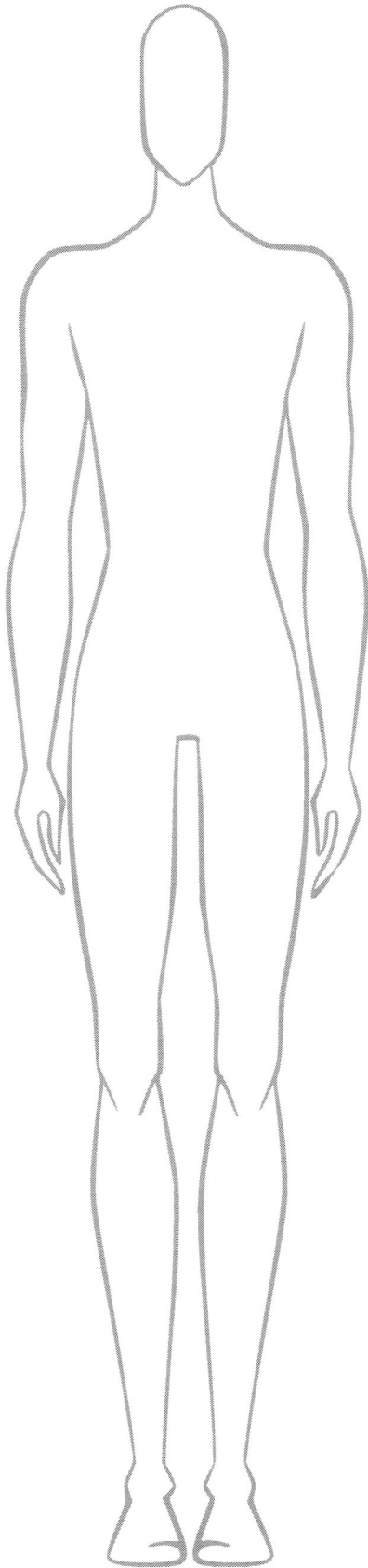

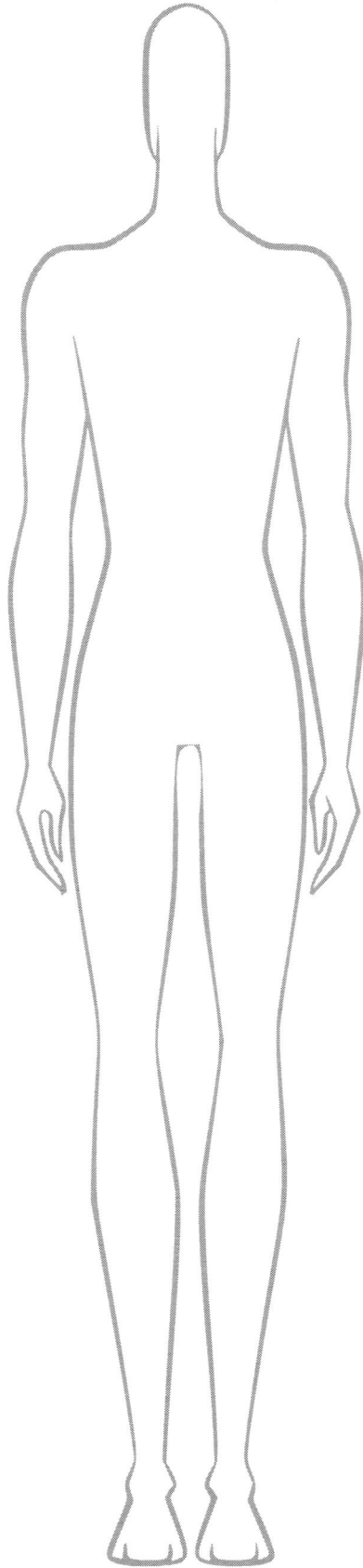

NOTES

NOTES

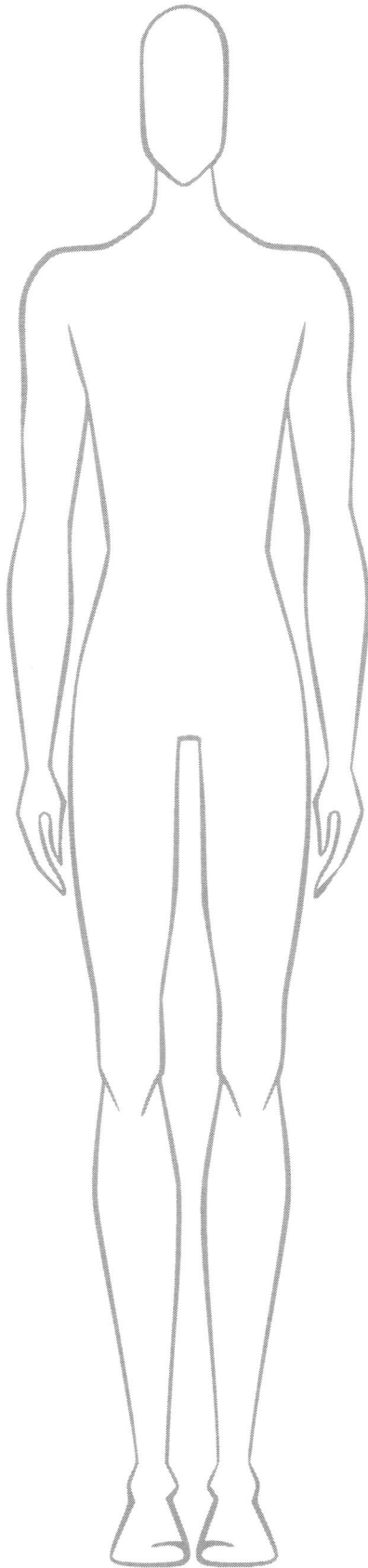

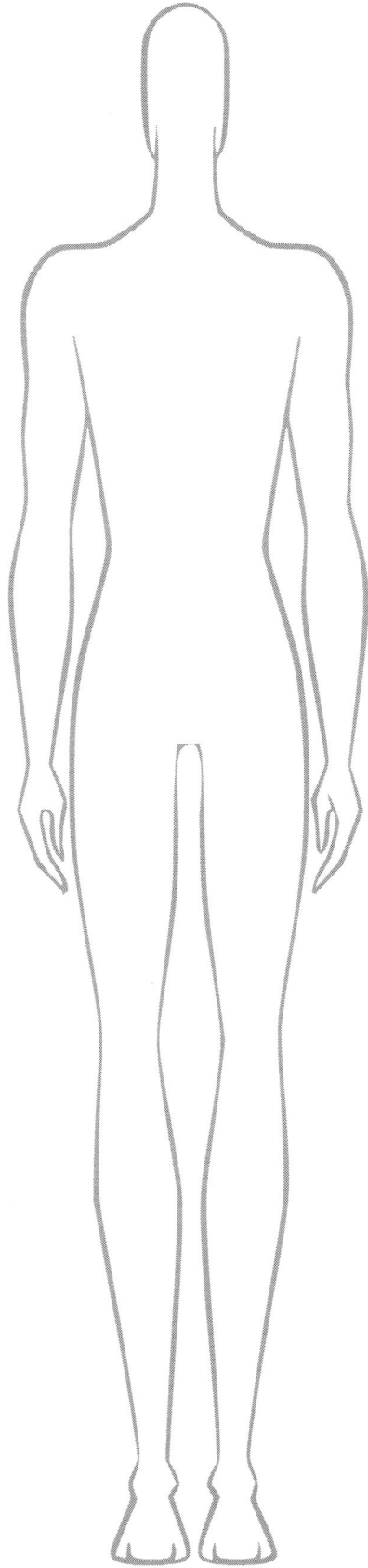

NOTES

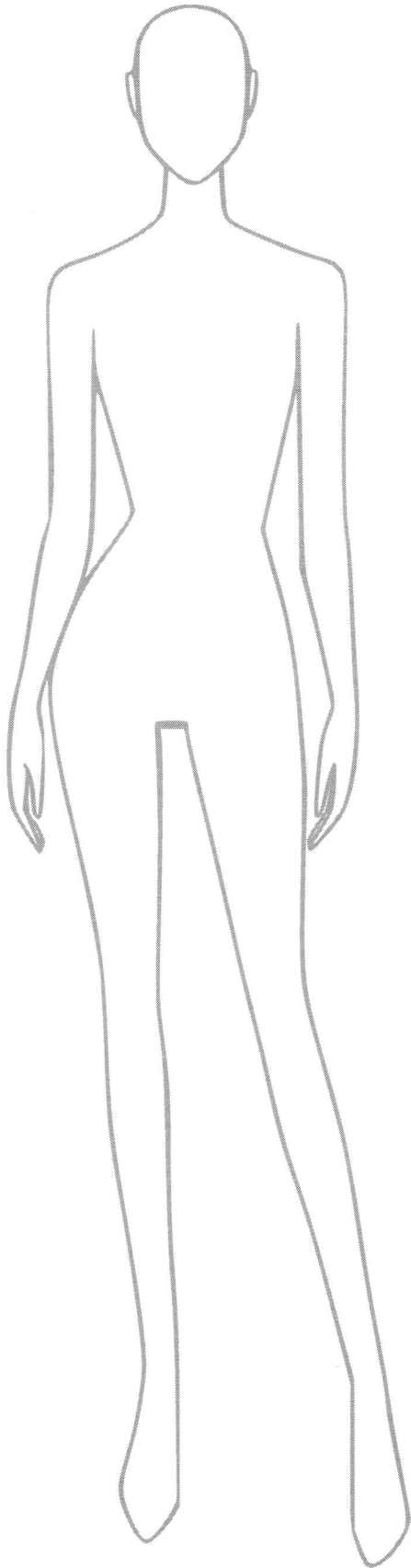

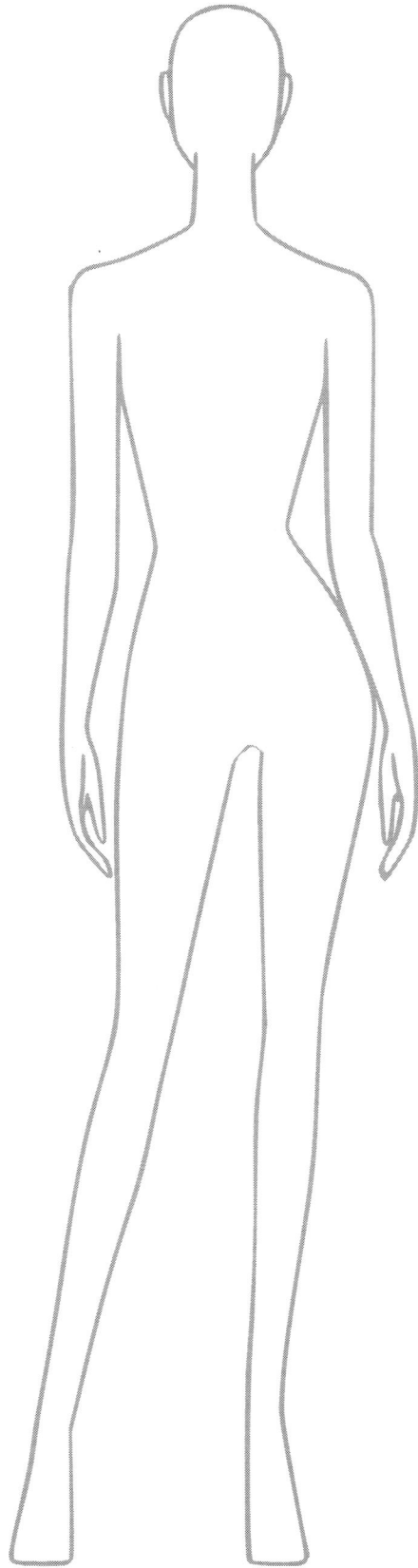

NOTES

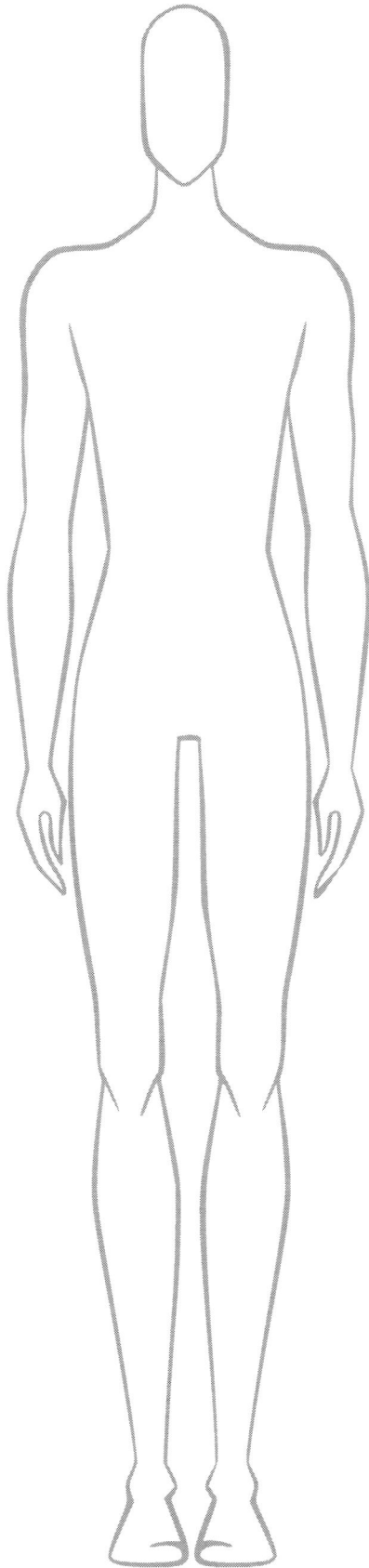

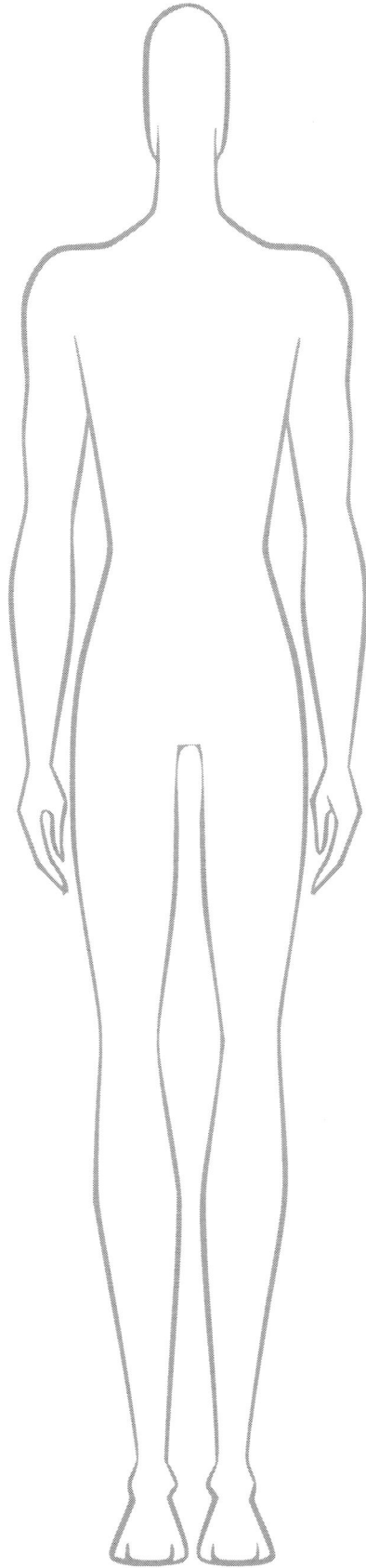

NOTES

NOTES

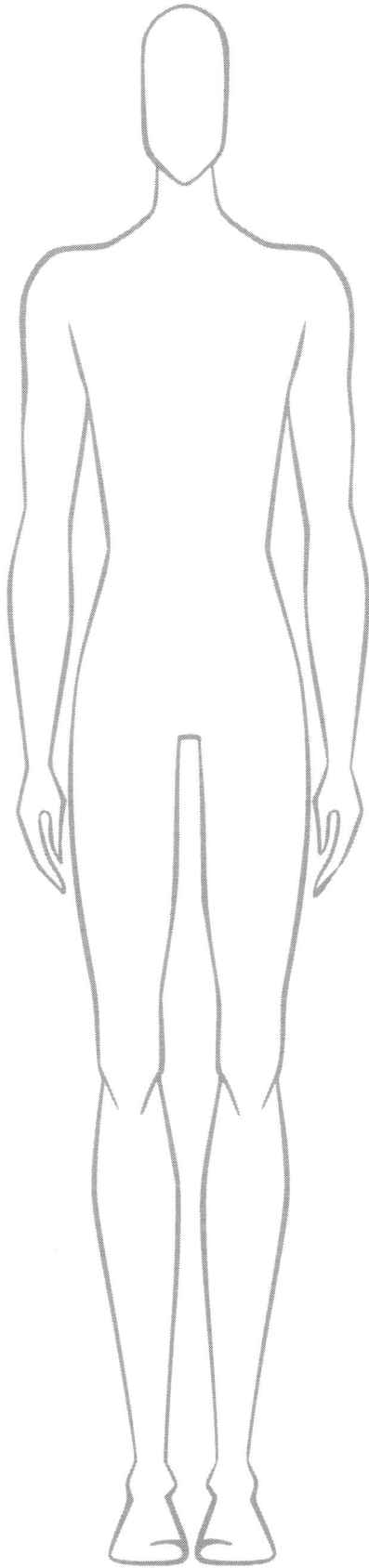

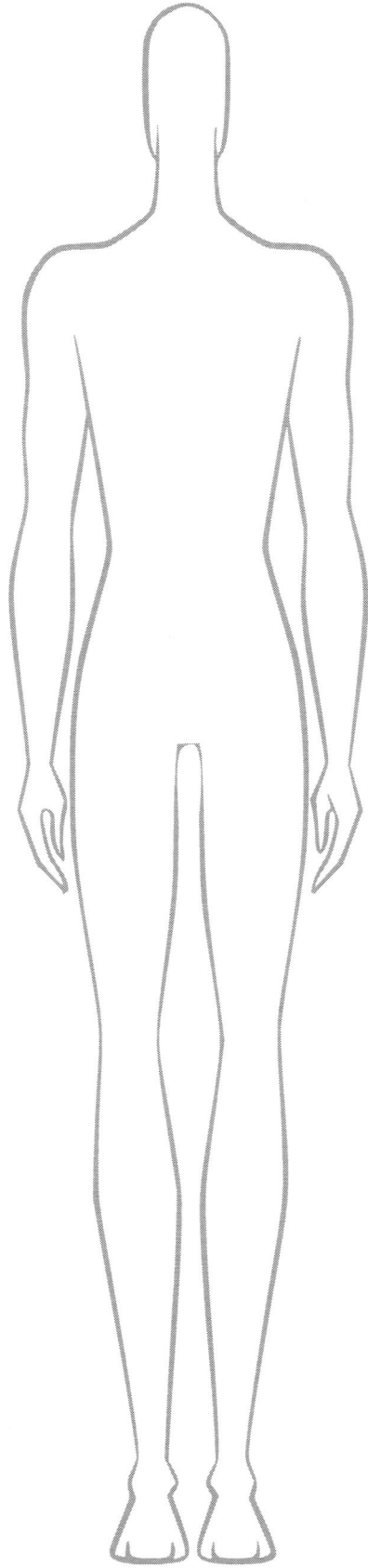

NOTES

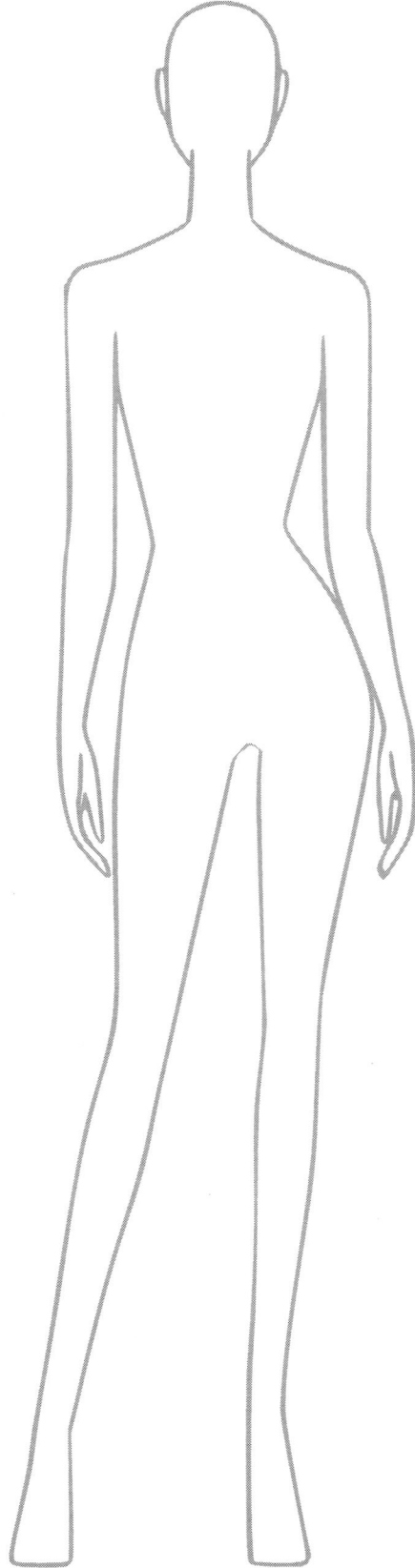

NOTES

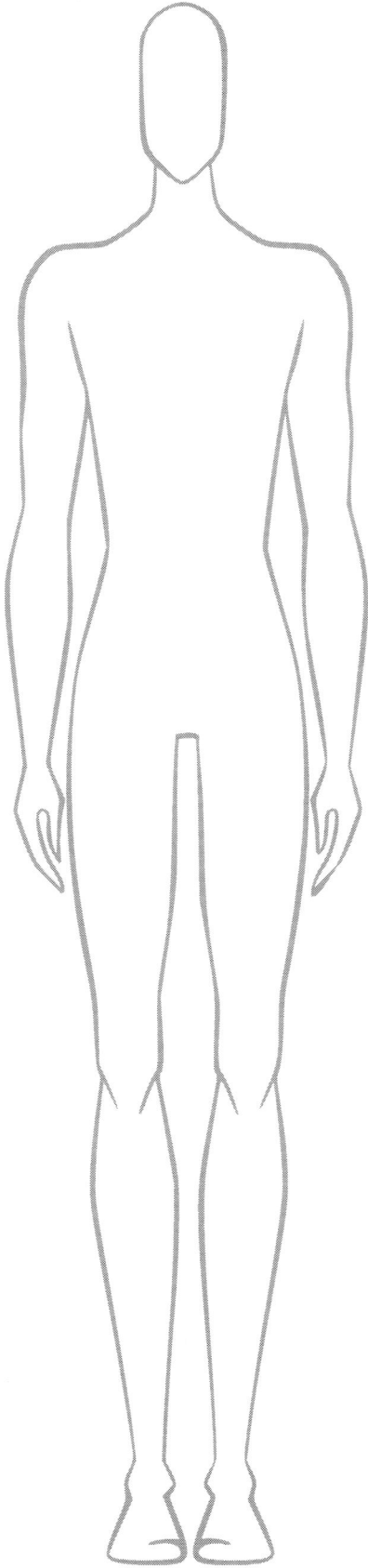

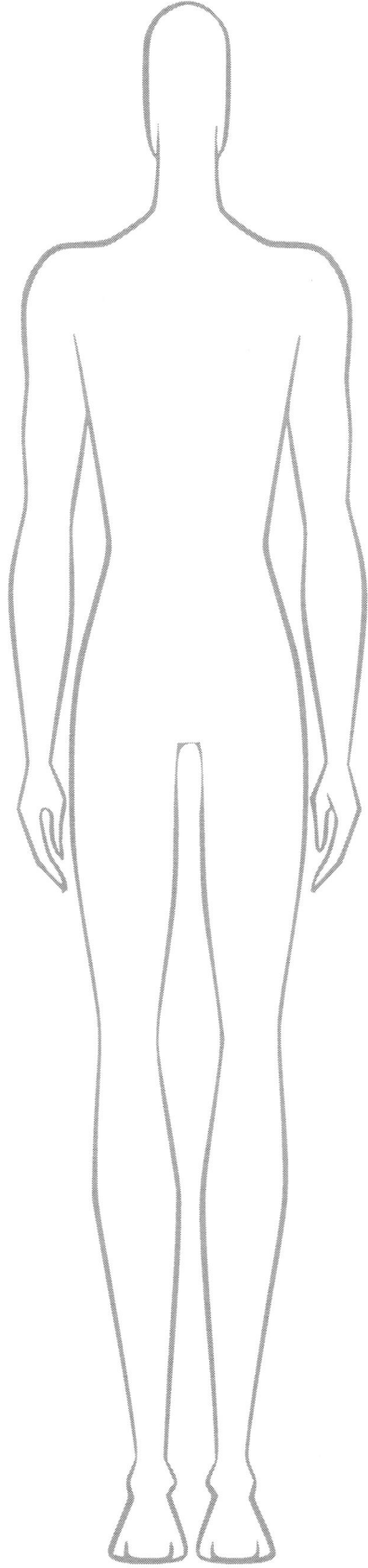

NOTES

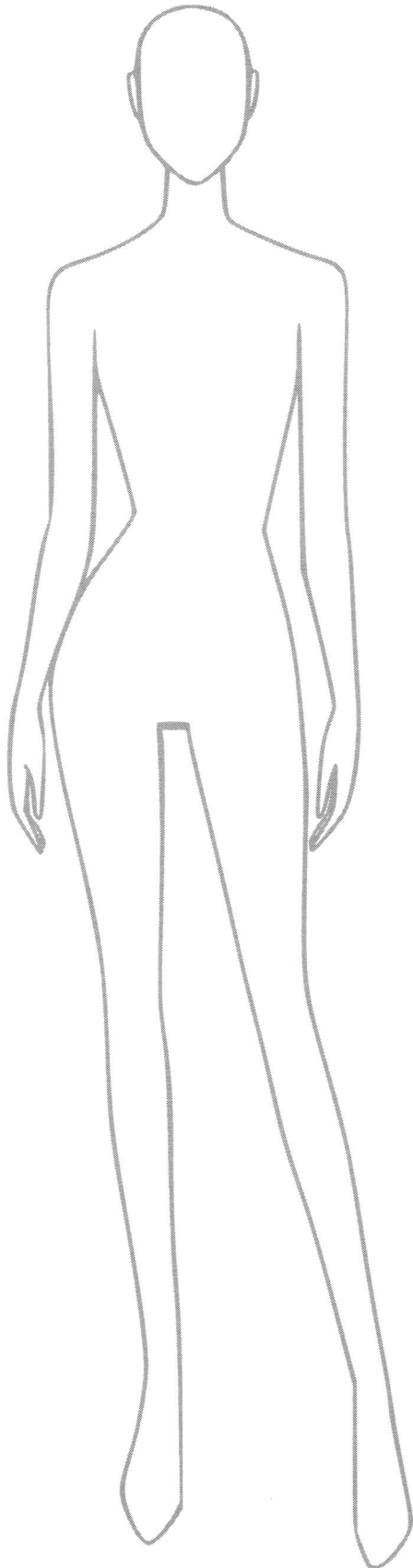

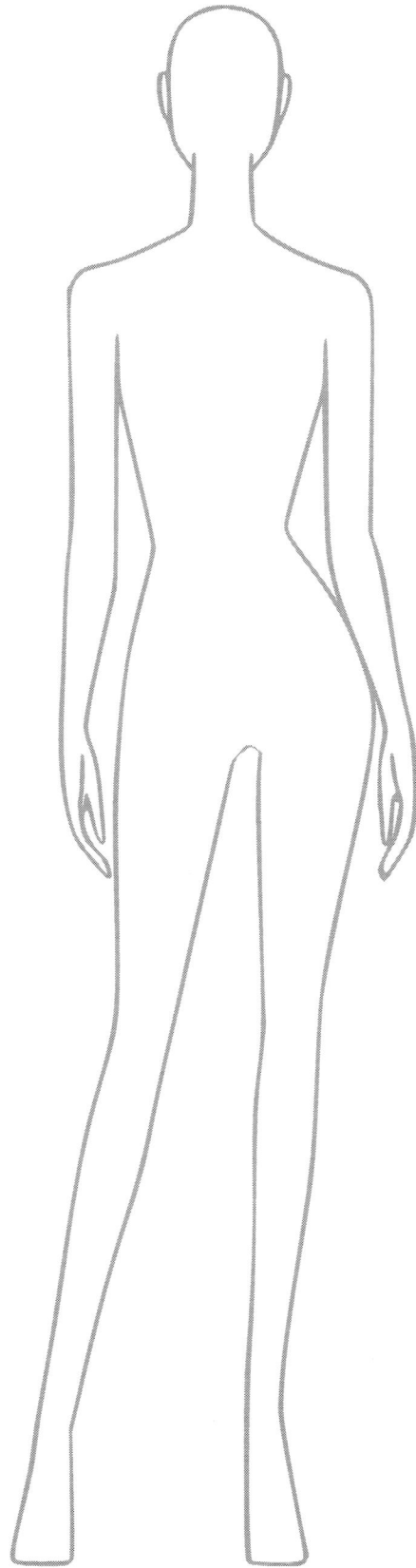

NOTES

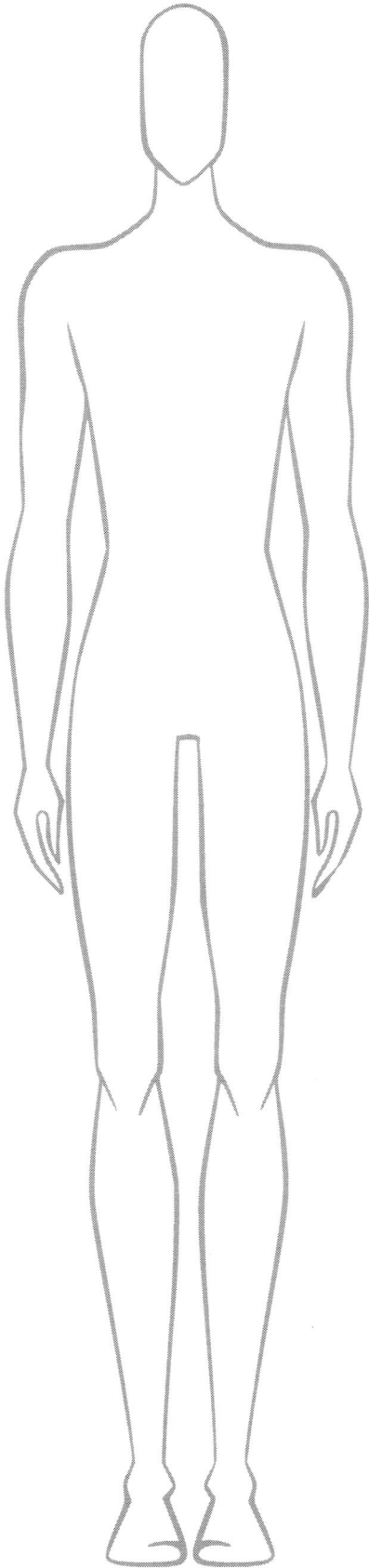

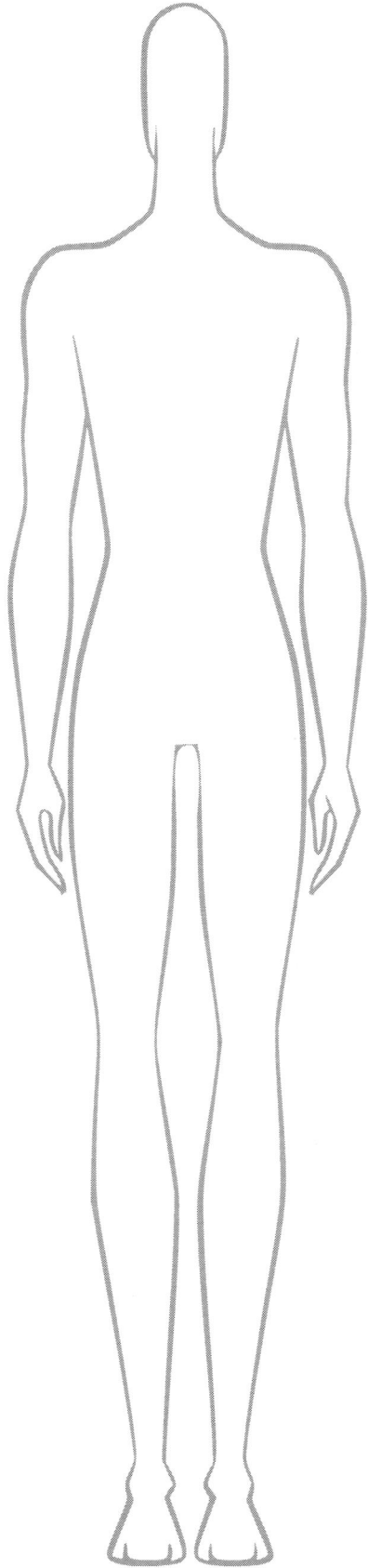

NOTES

NOTES

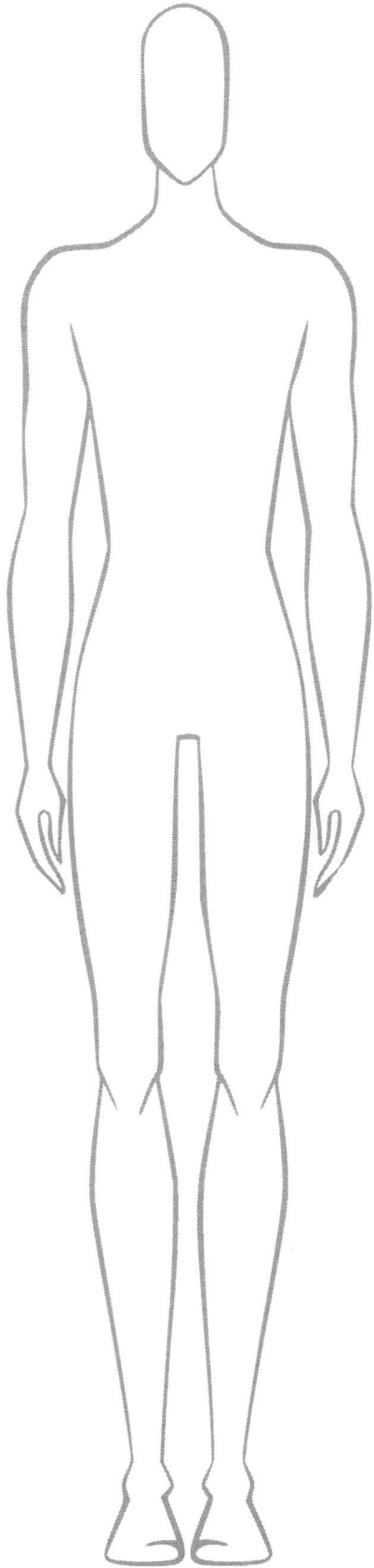

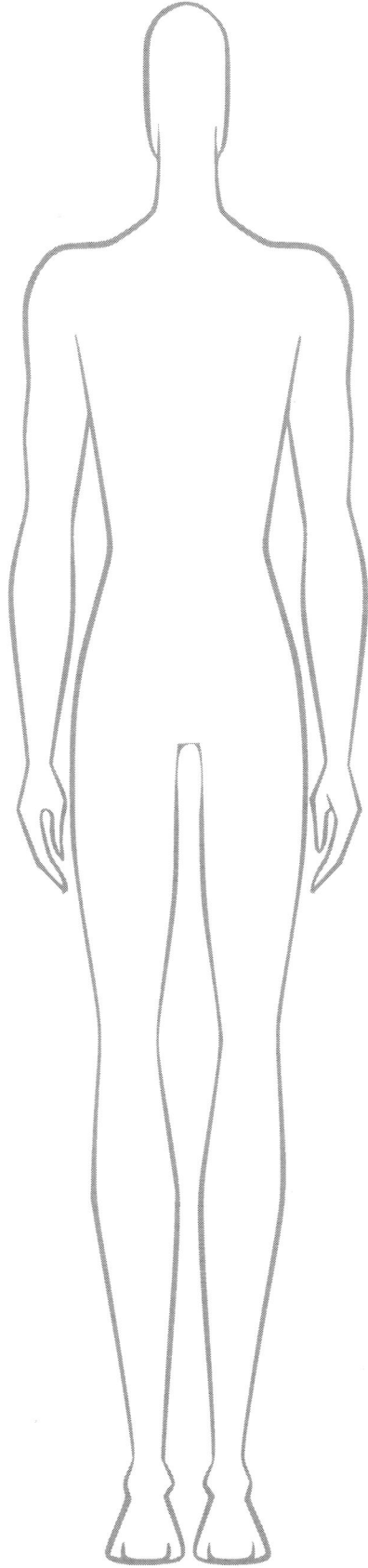

NOTES

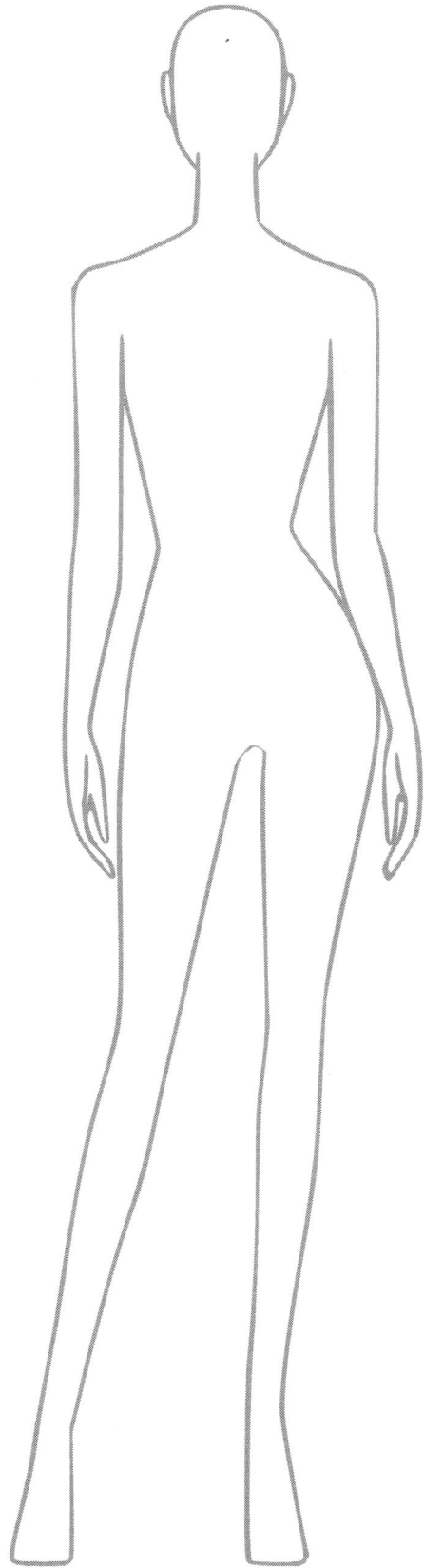

NOTES

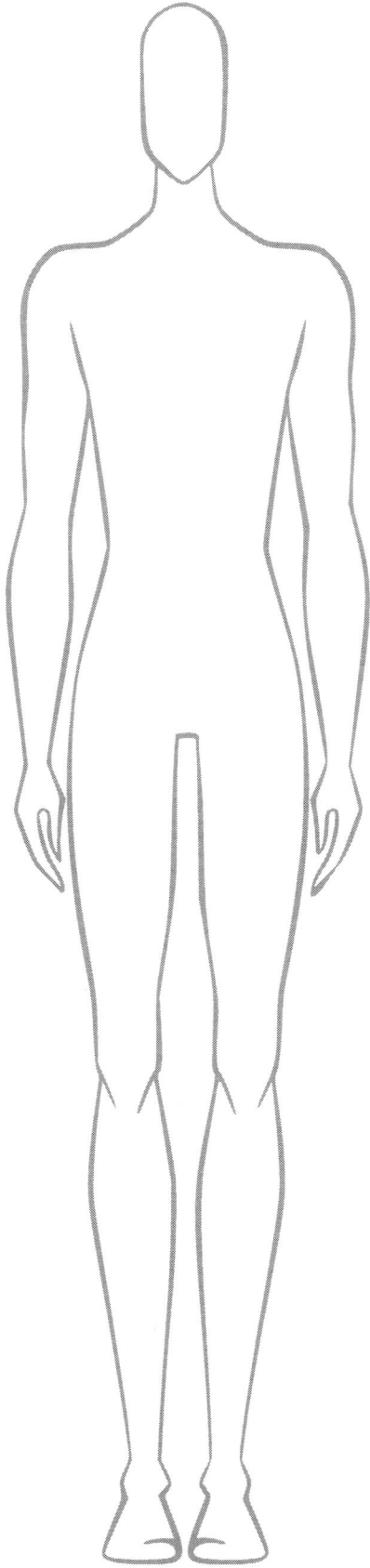

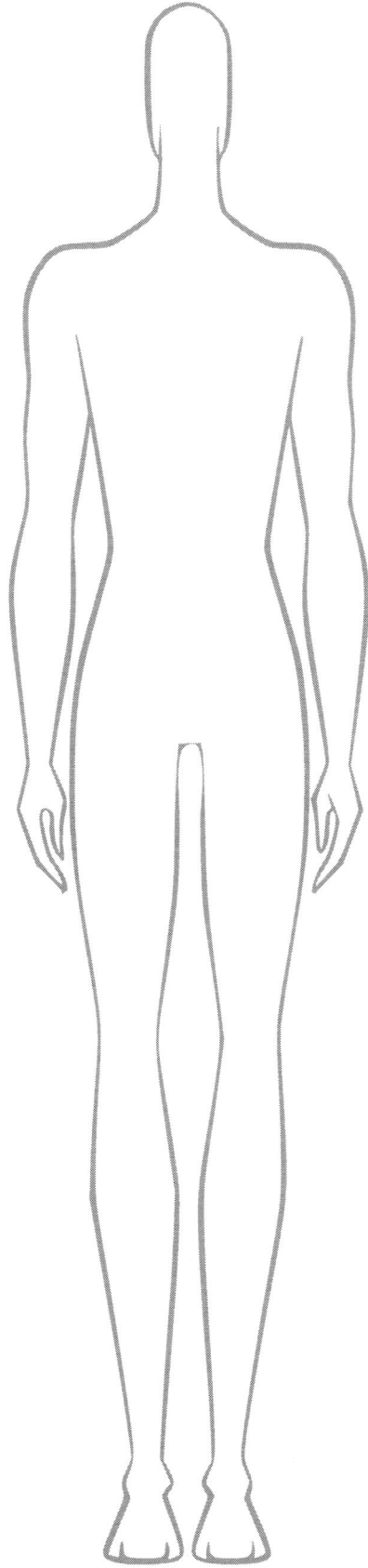

NOTES

NOTES

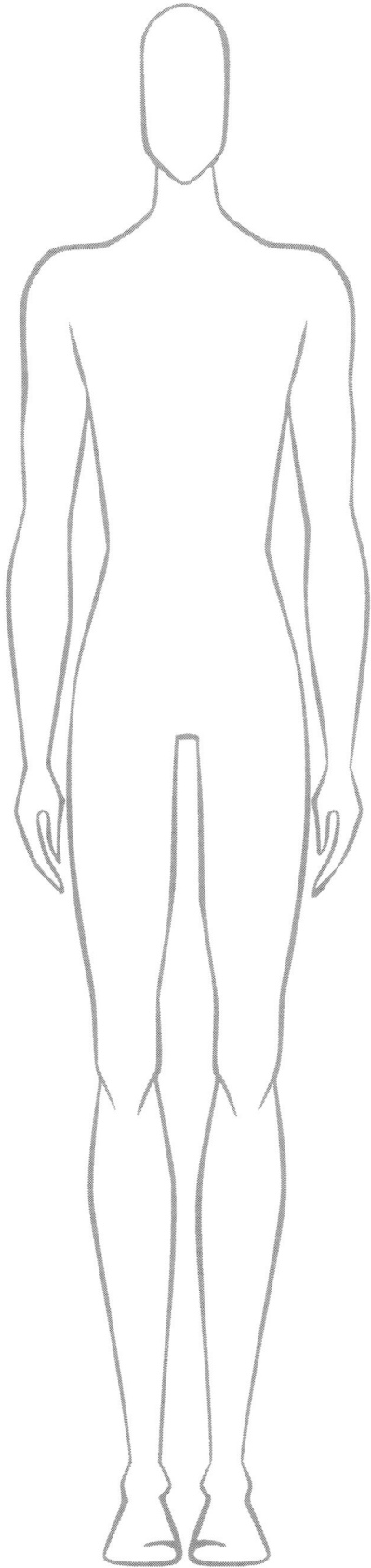

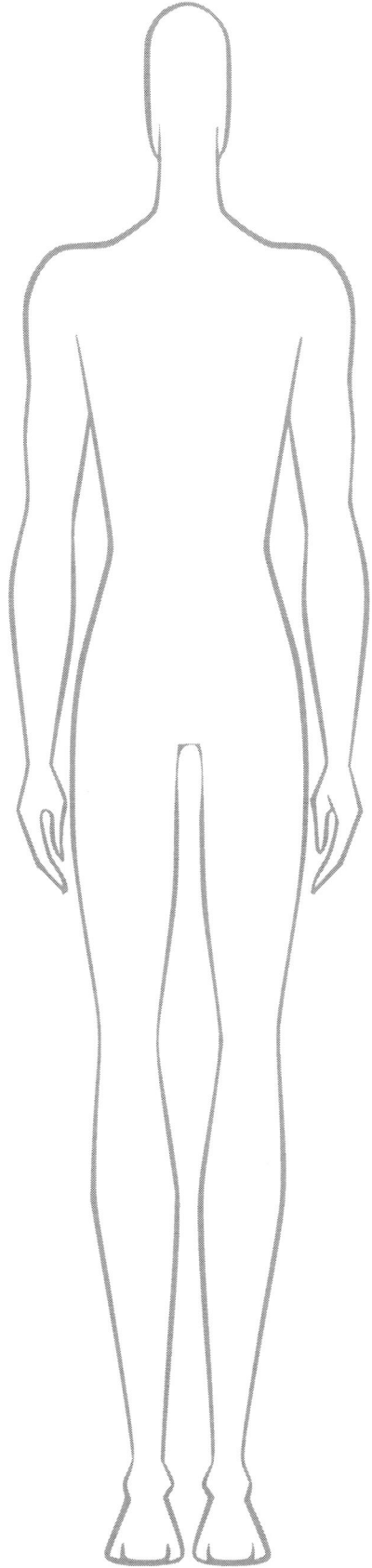

NOTES

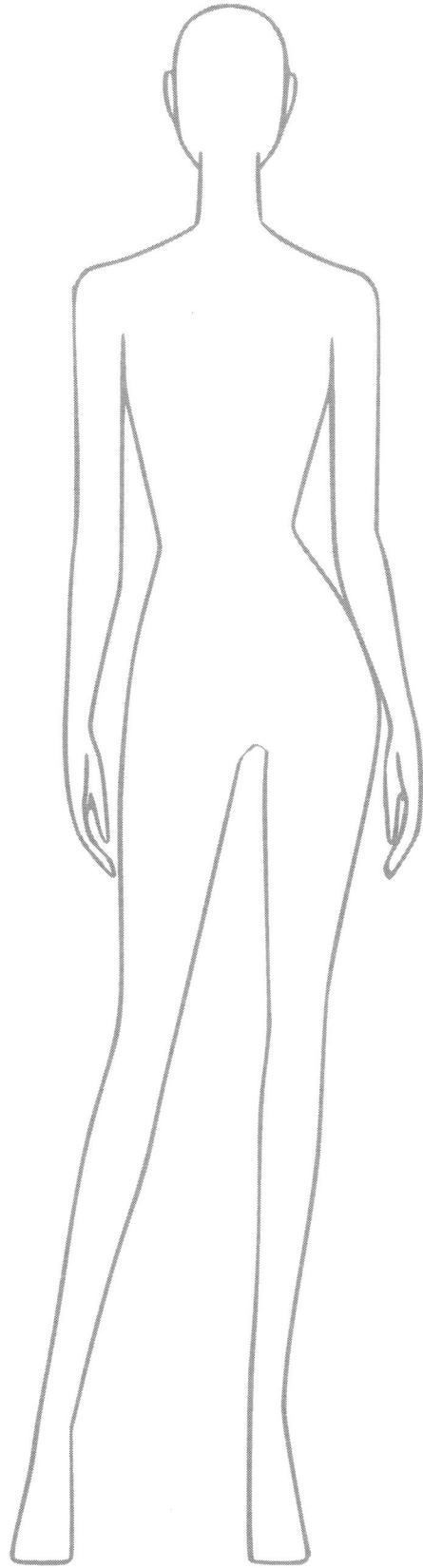

NOTES

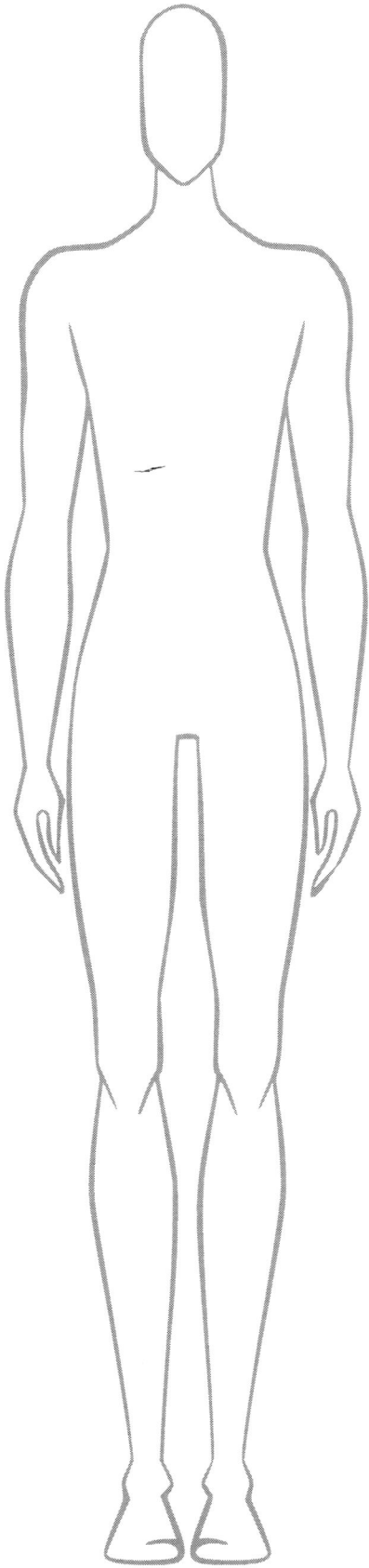

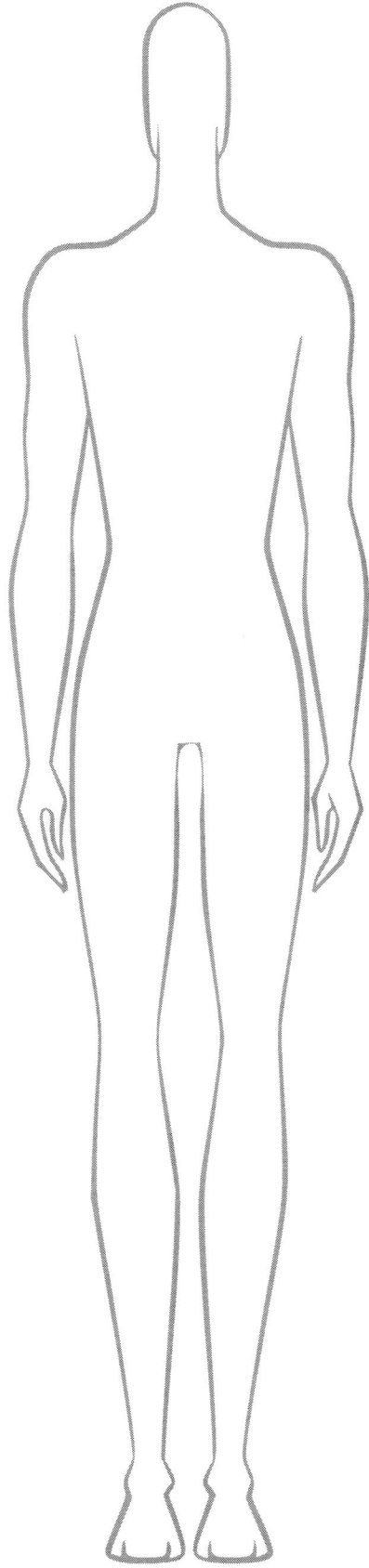

NOTES

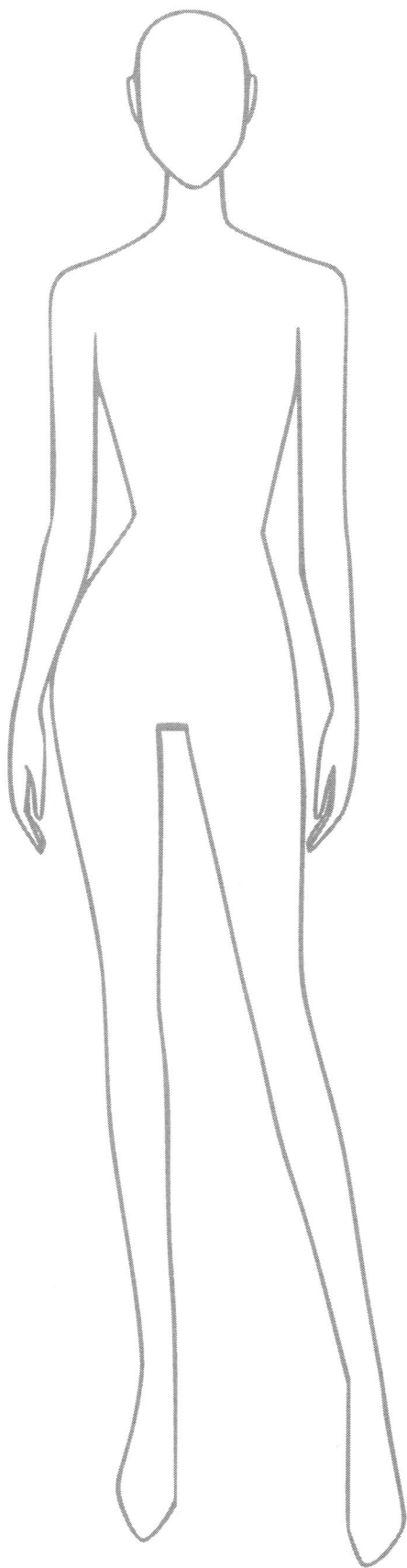

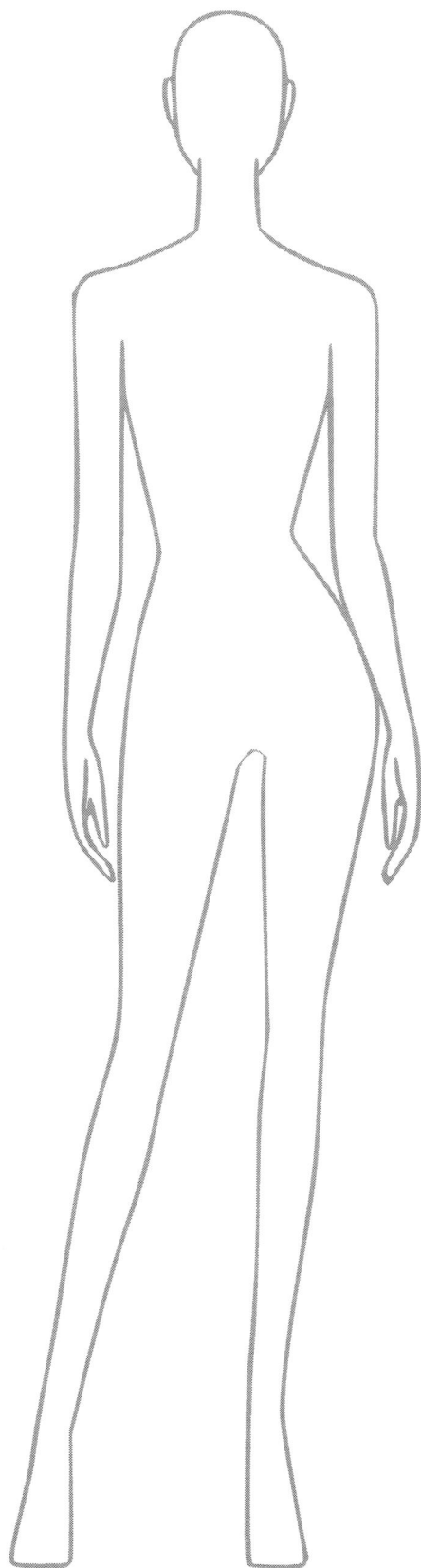

NOTES

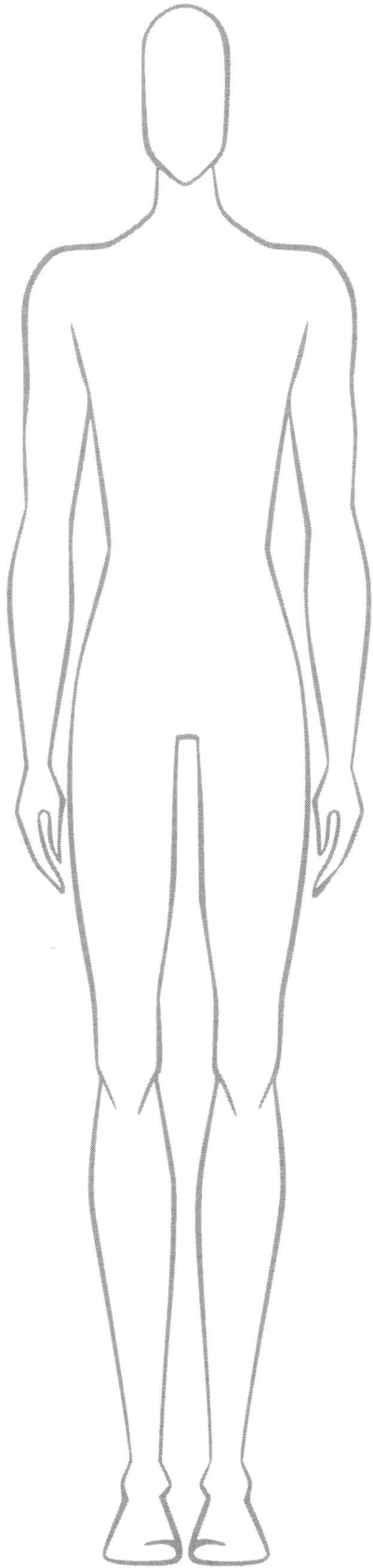

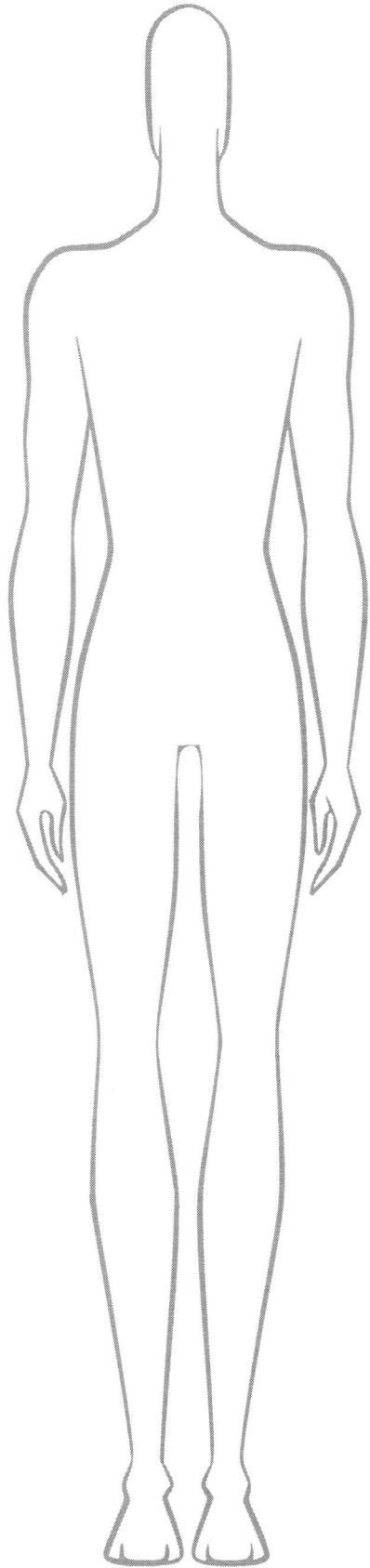

NOTES

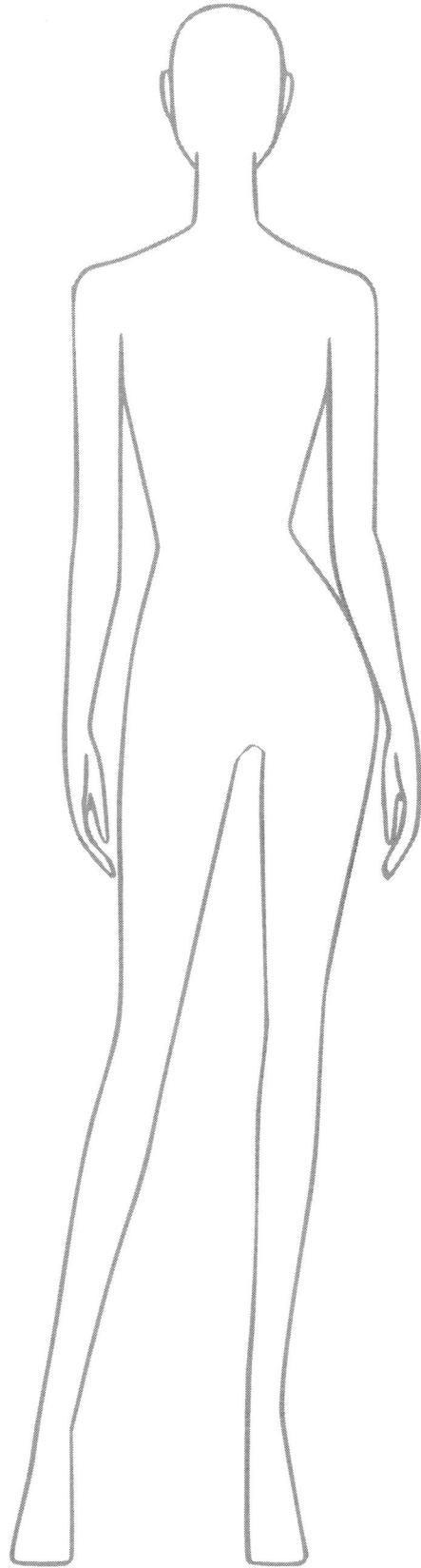

NOTES

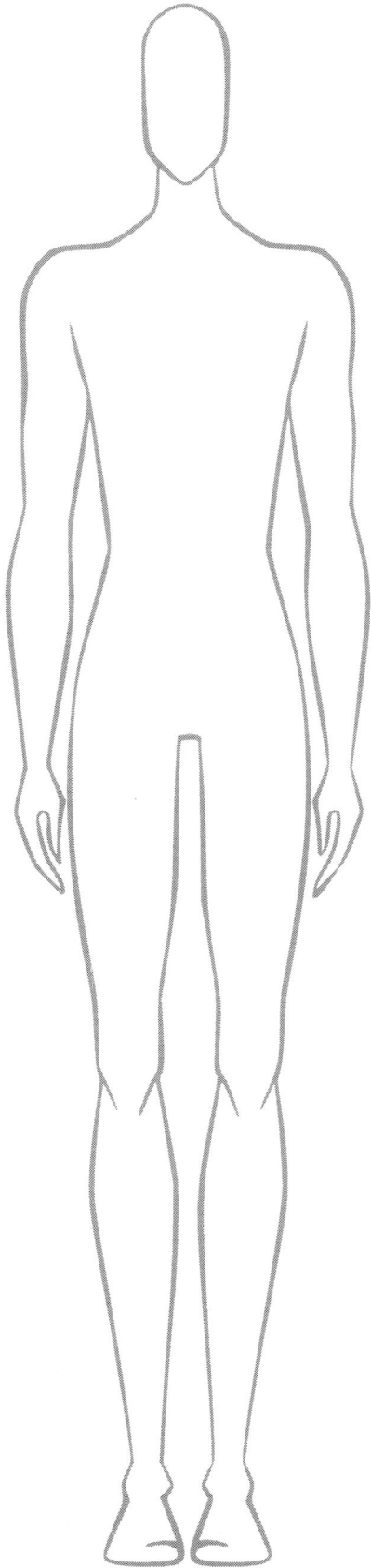

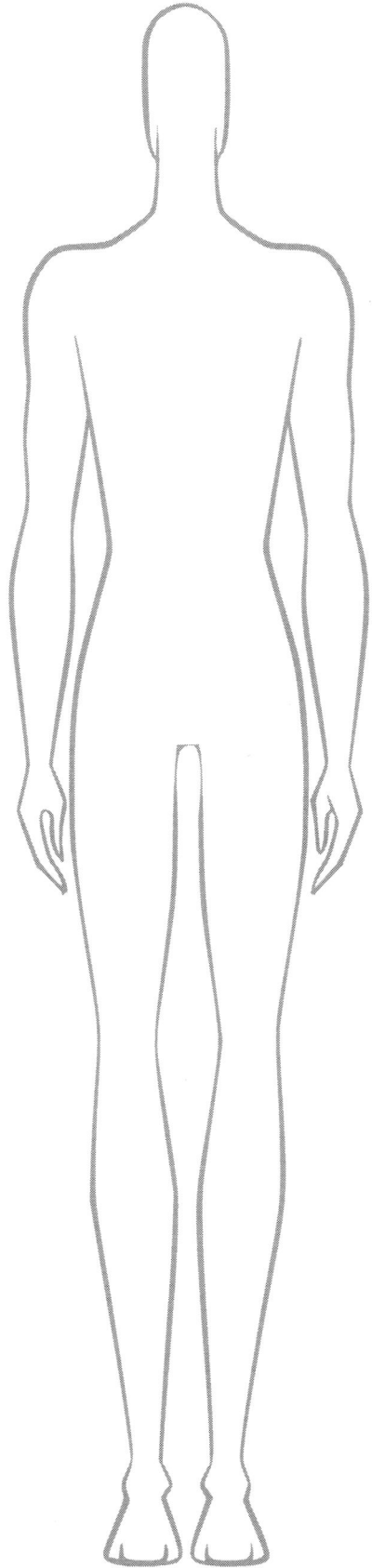

NOTES

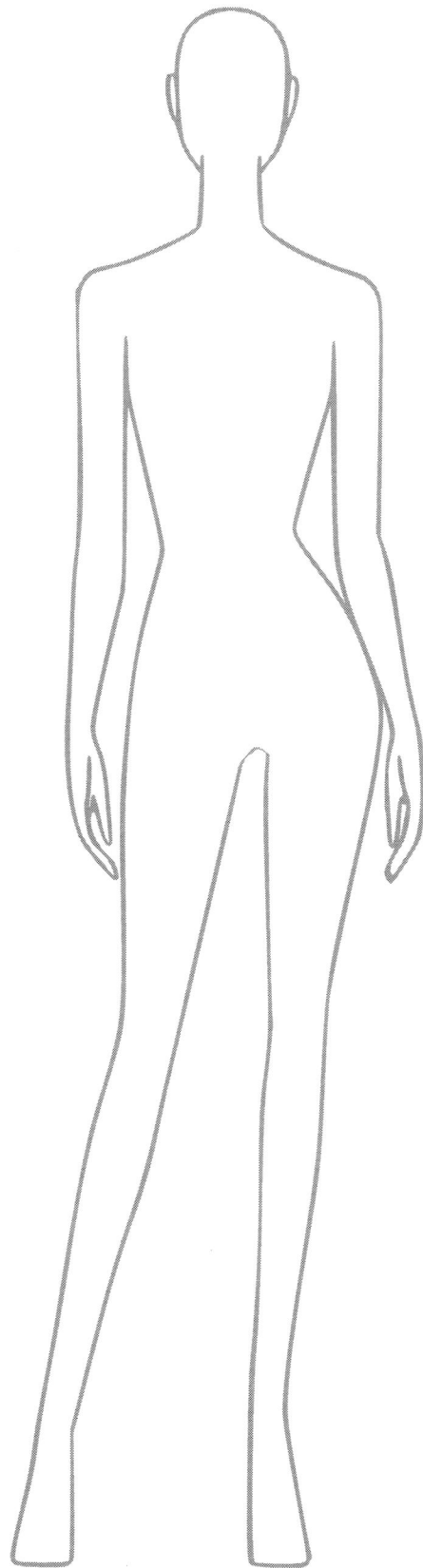

NOTES

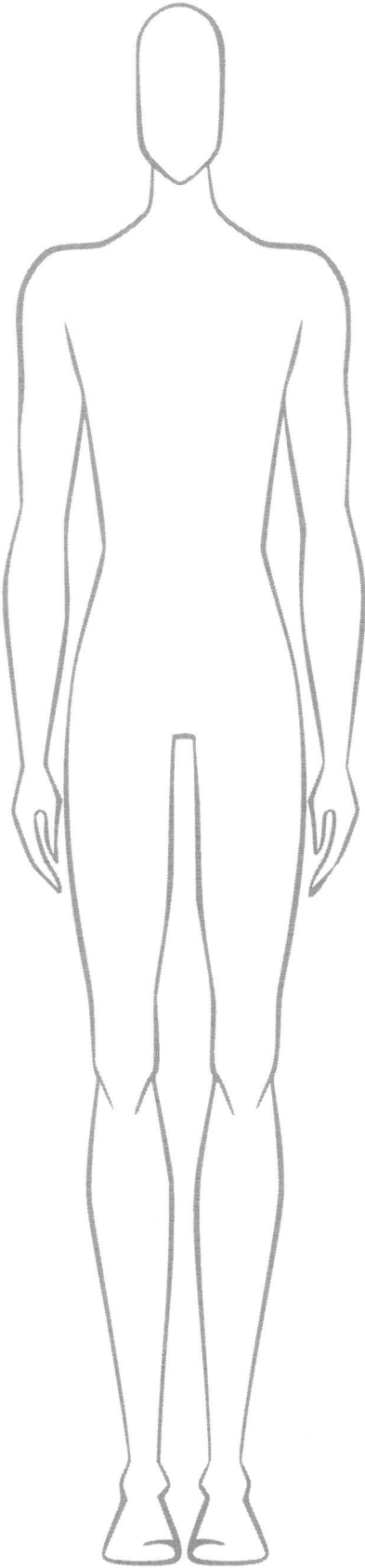

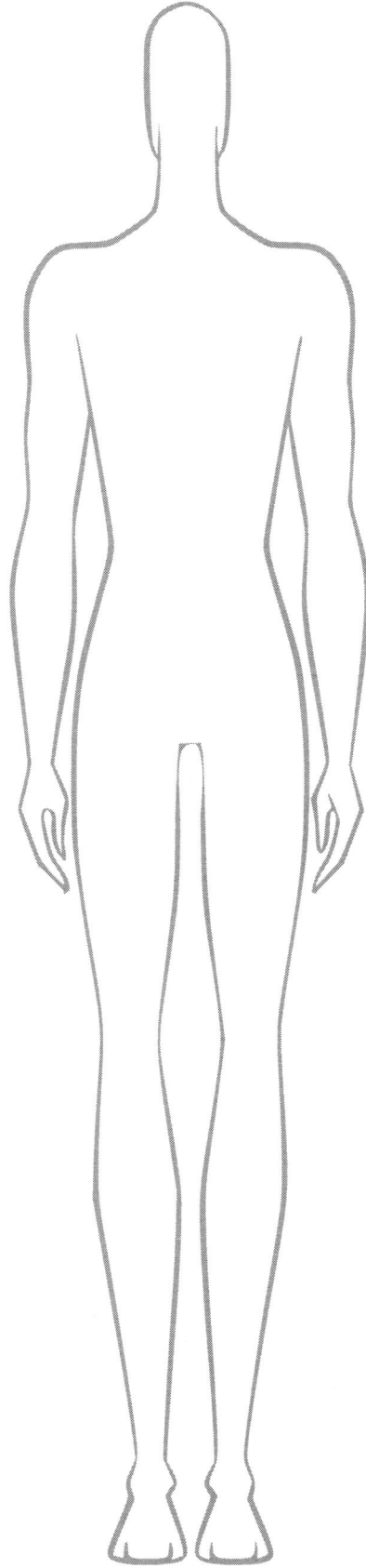

NOTES

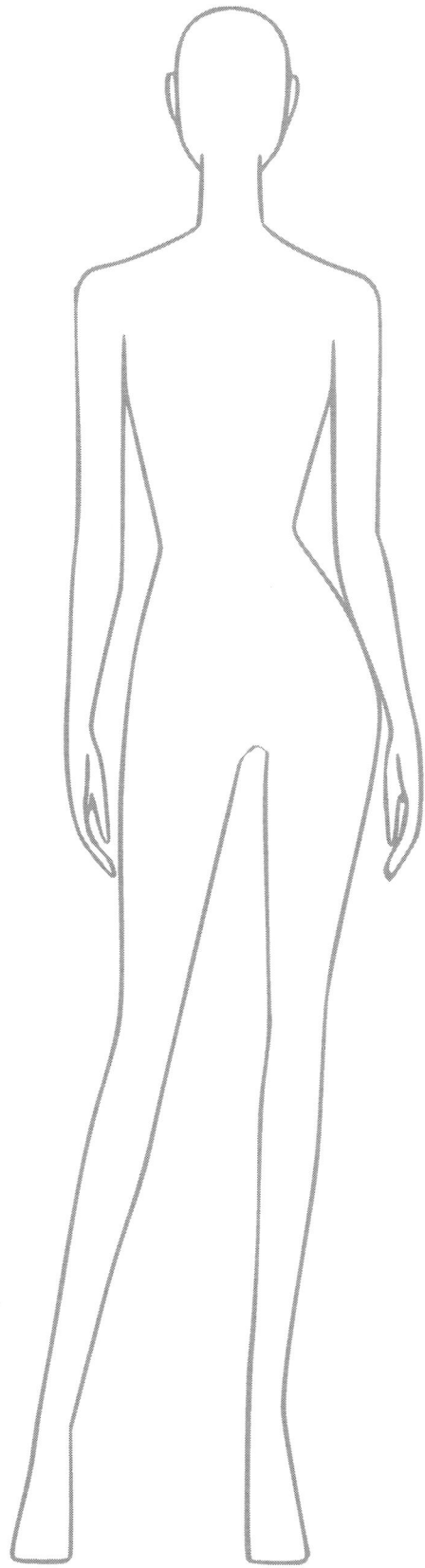

NOTES

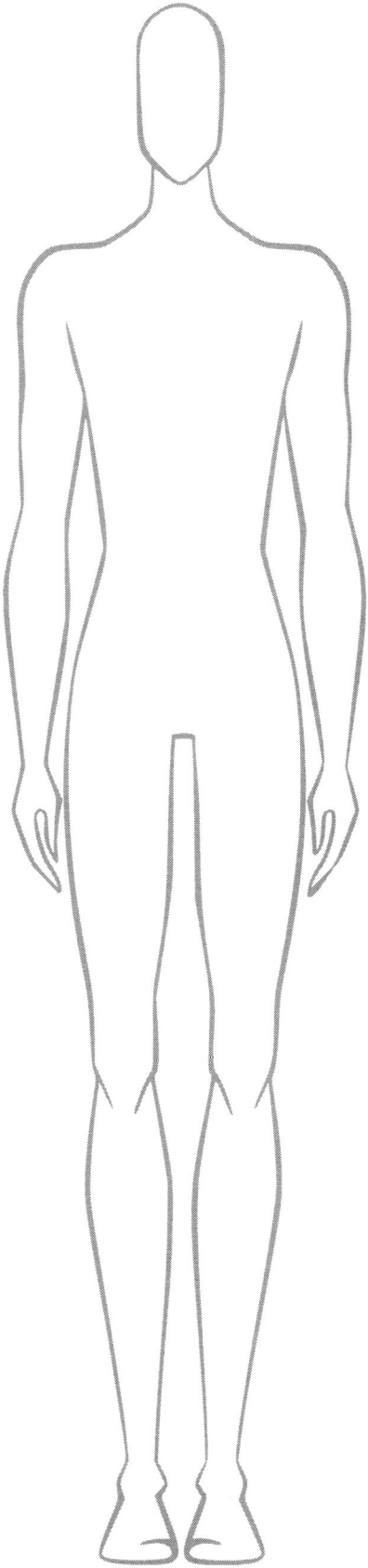

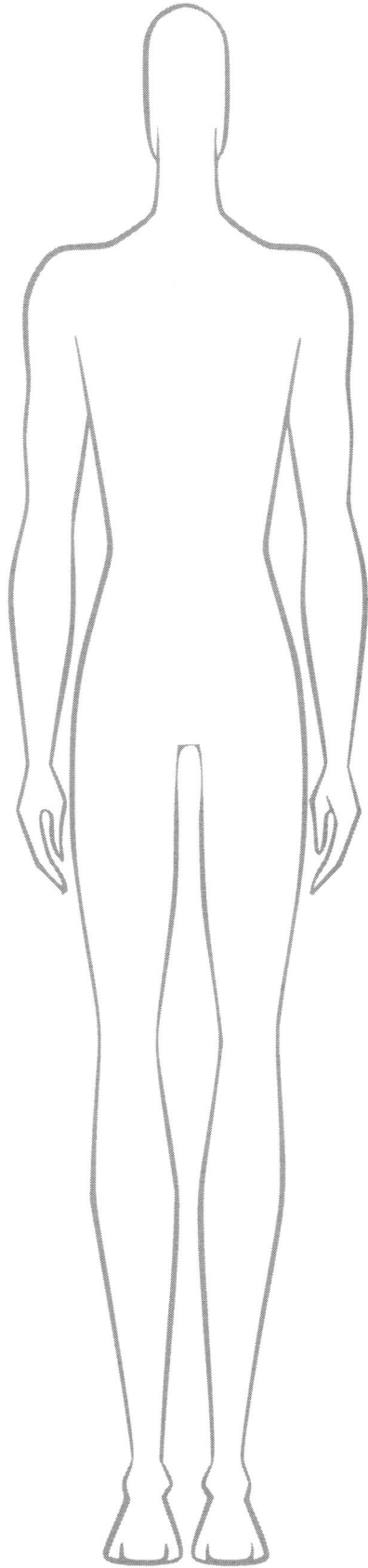

NOTES

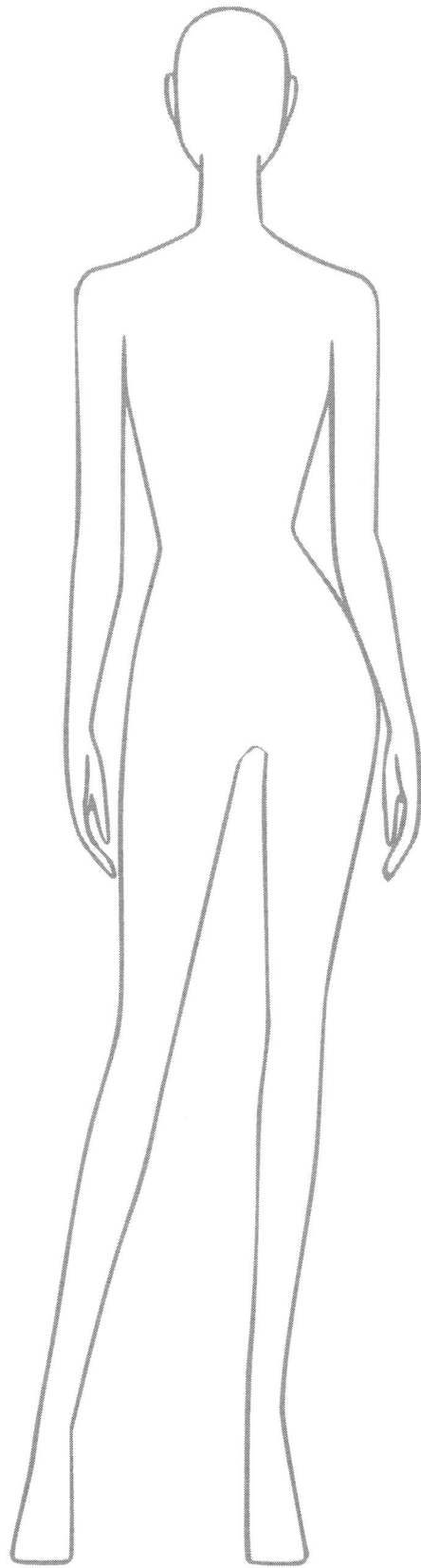

NOTES

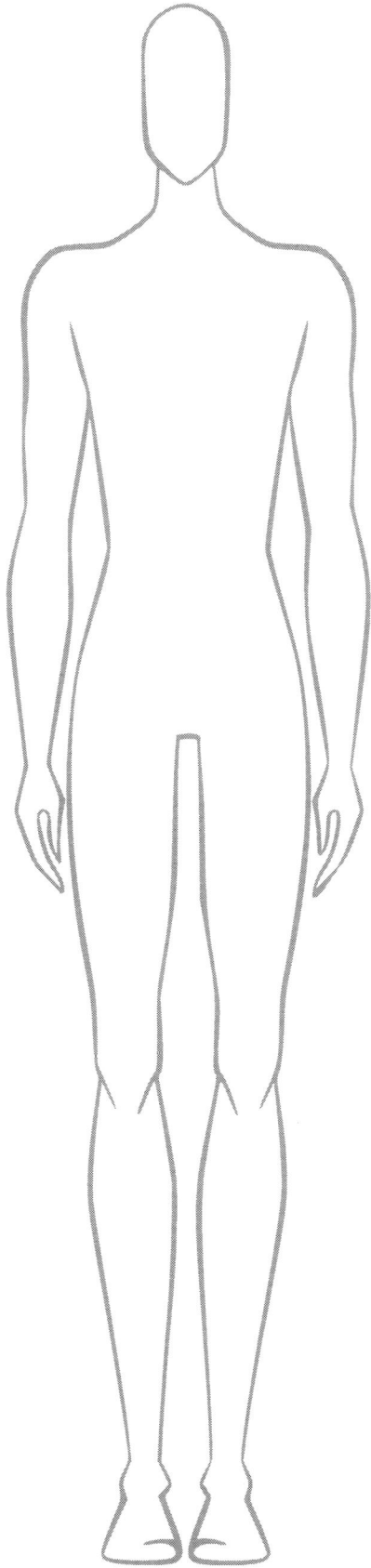

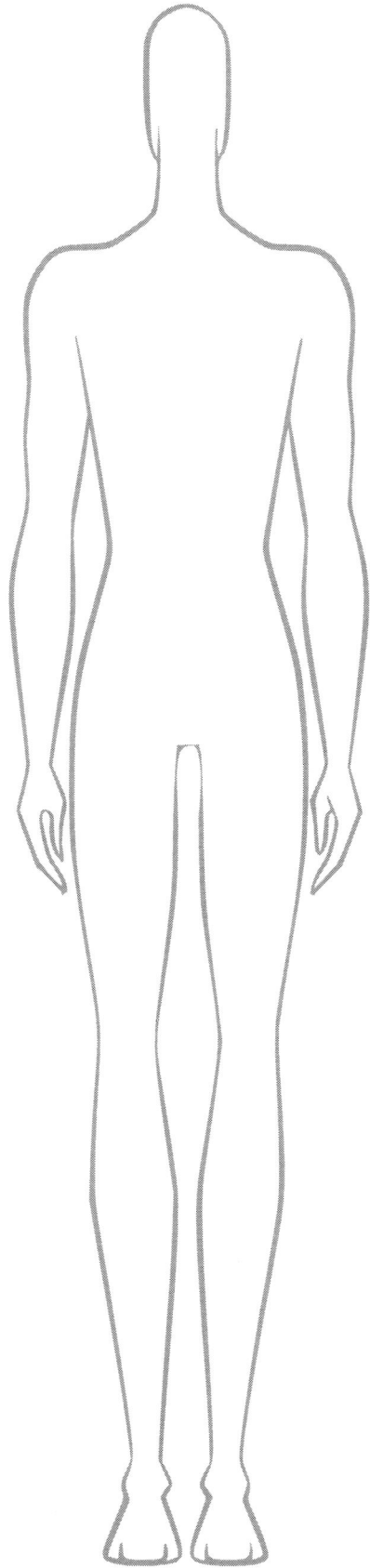

NOTES

NOTES

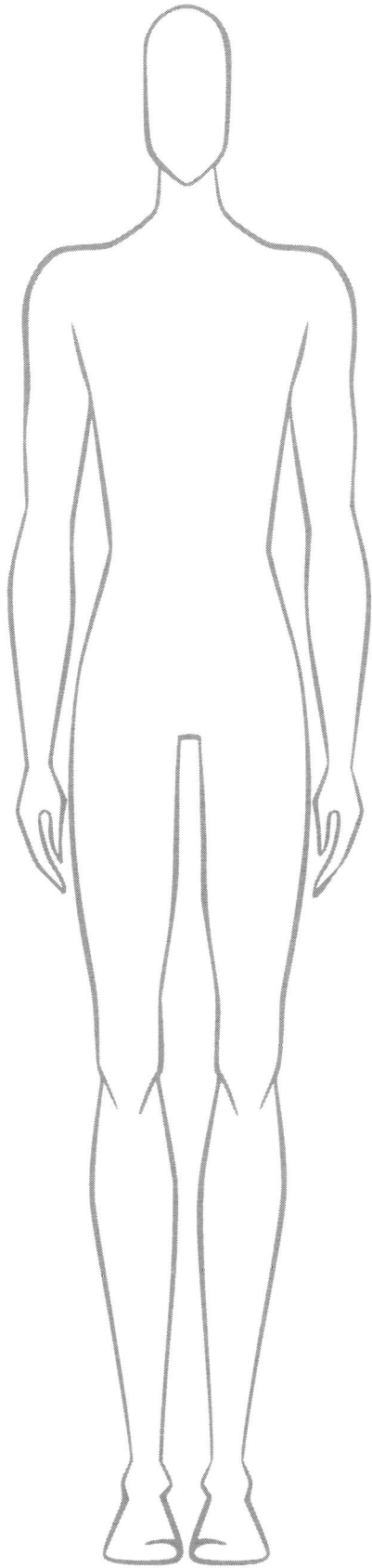

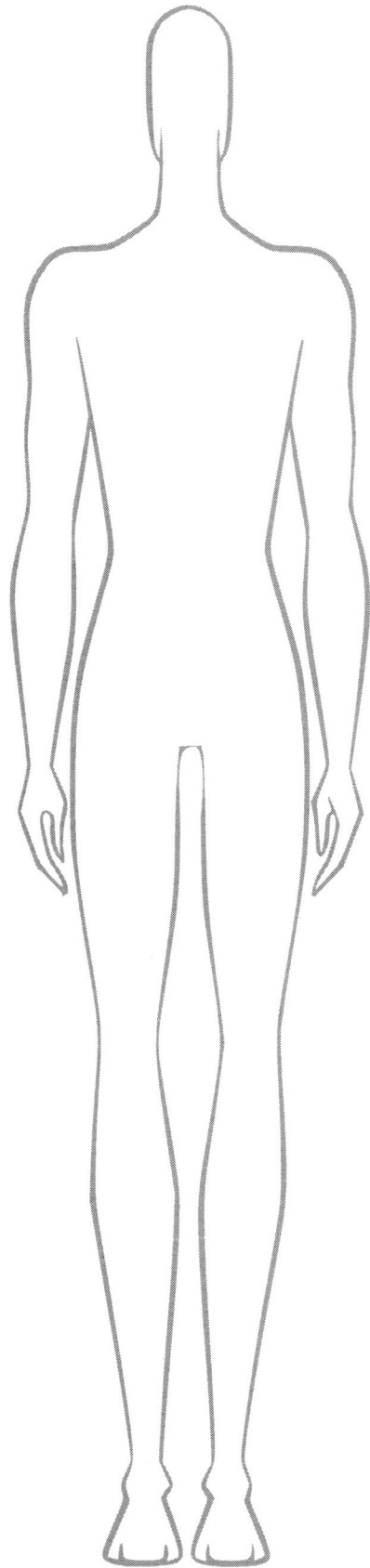

NOTES

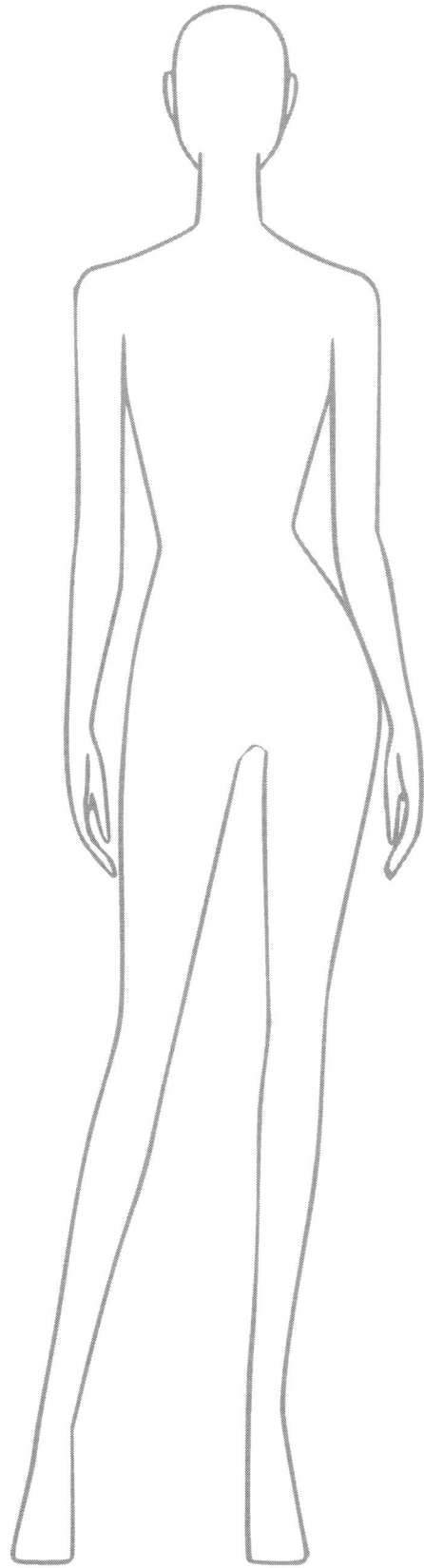

NOTES

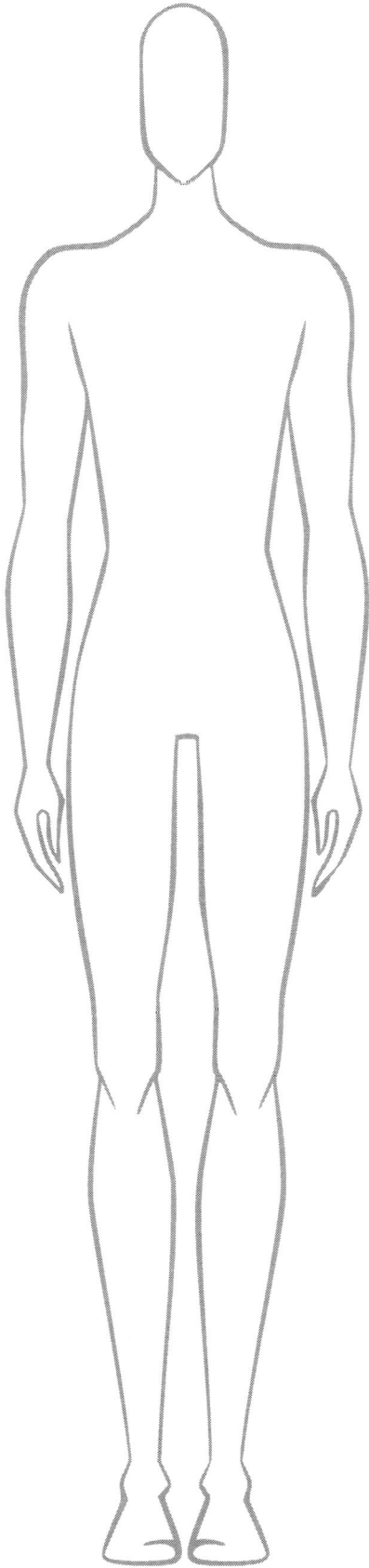

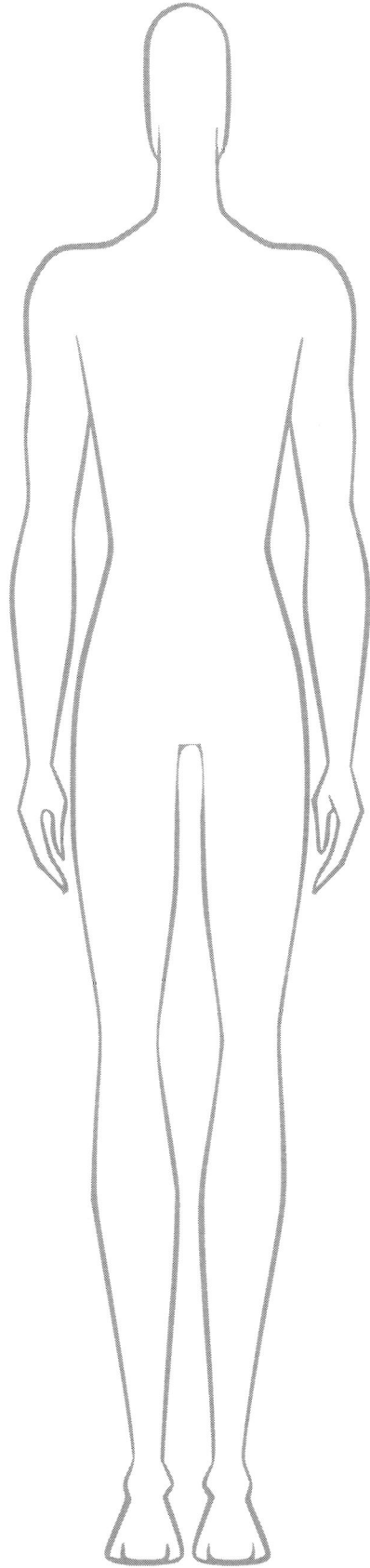

NOTES

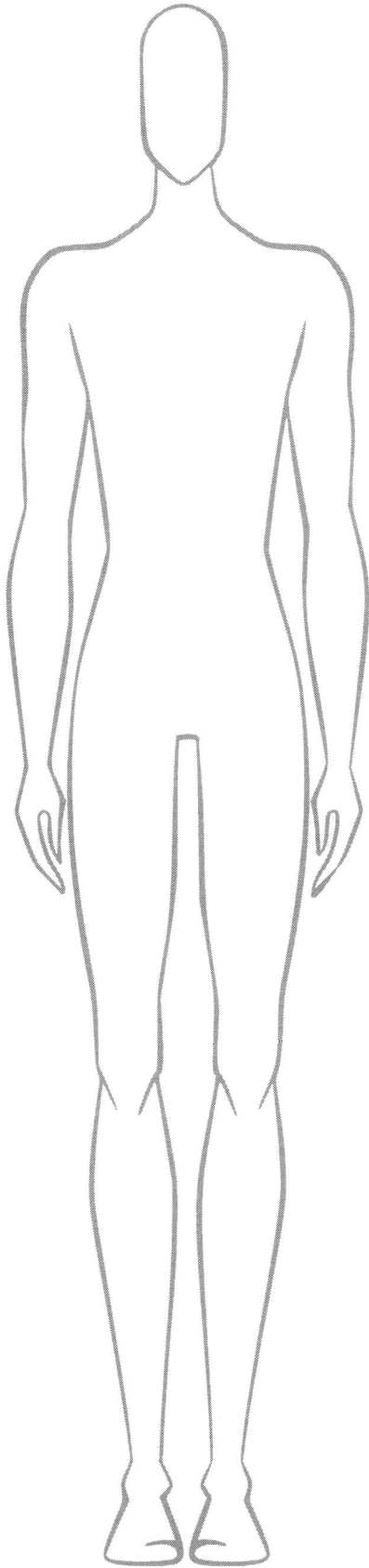

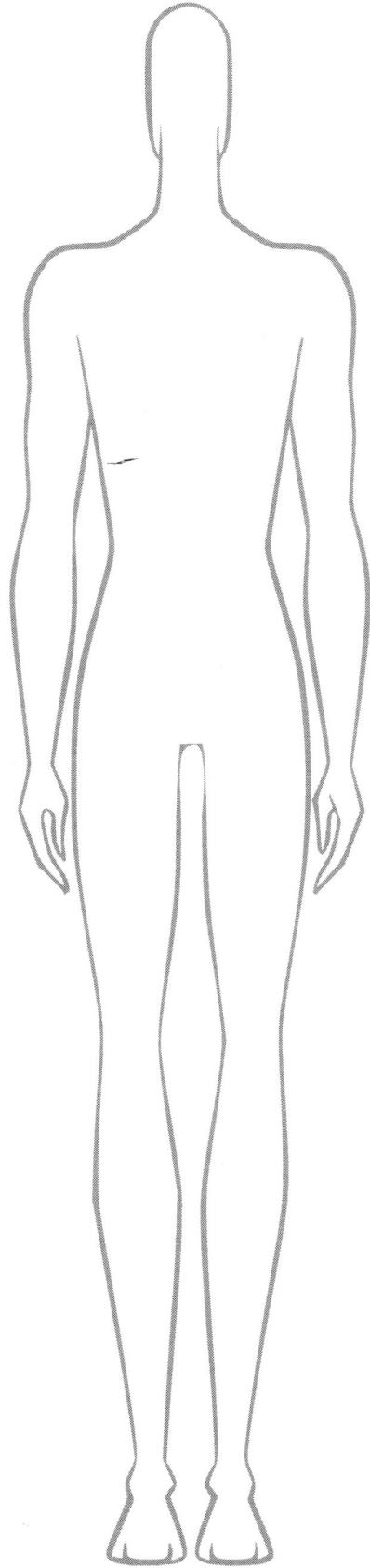

NOTES

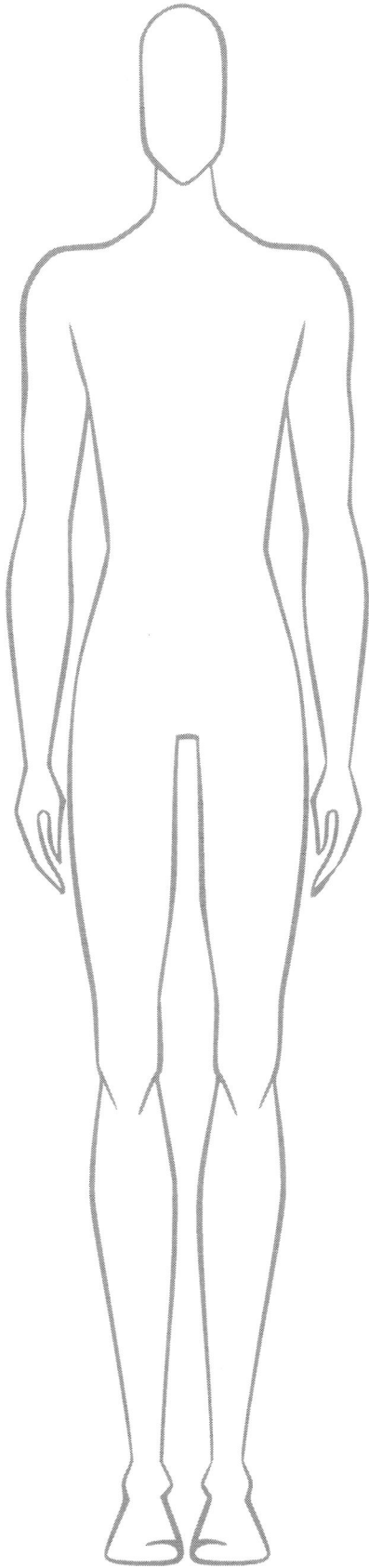

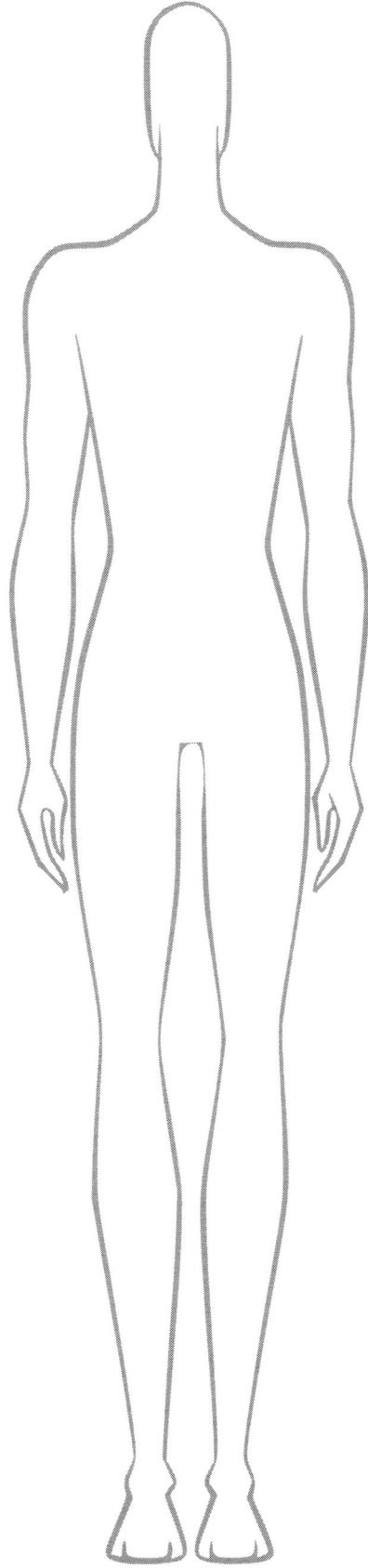

NOTES

NOTES

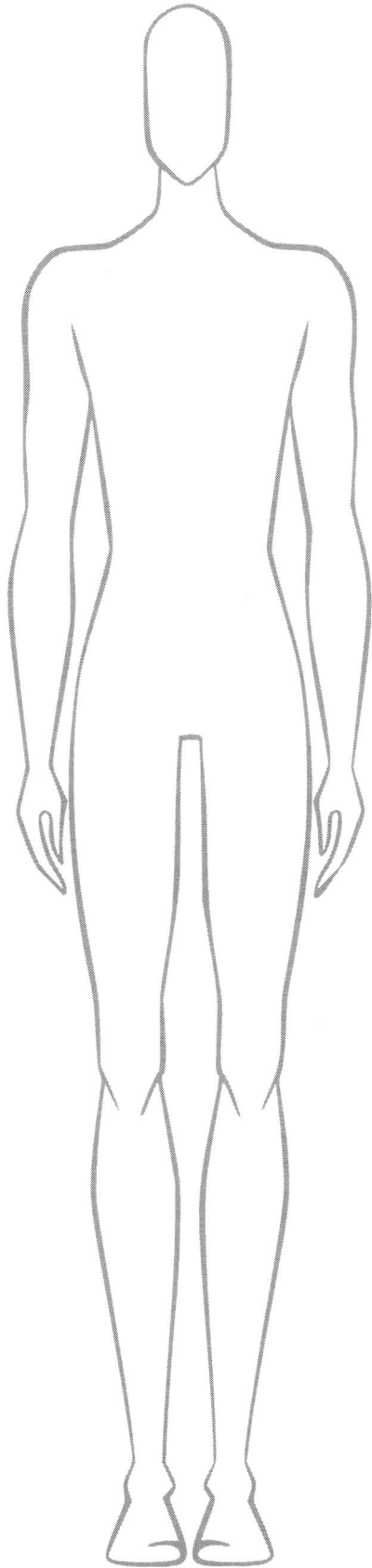

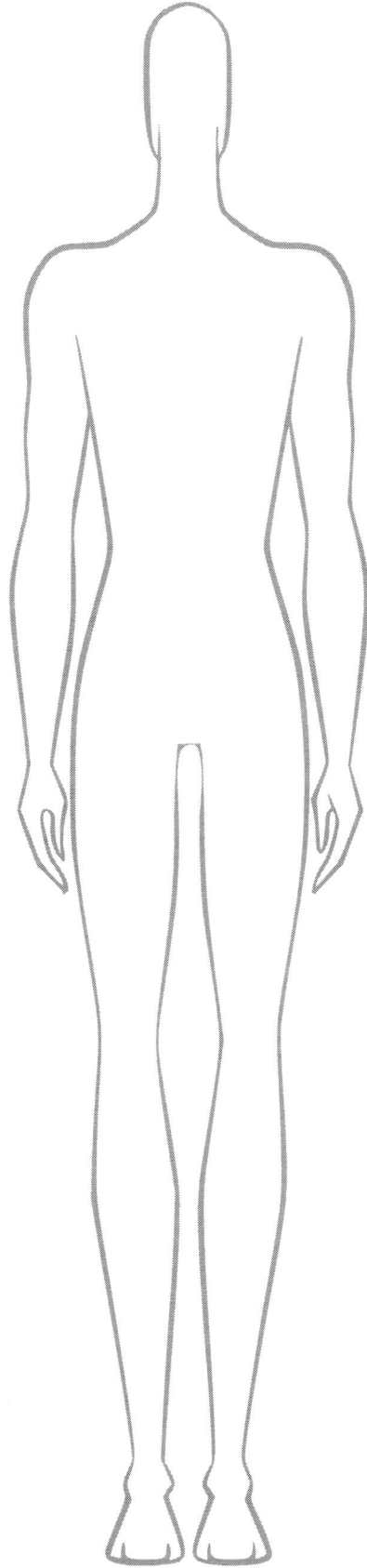

NOTES

NOTES

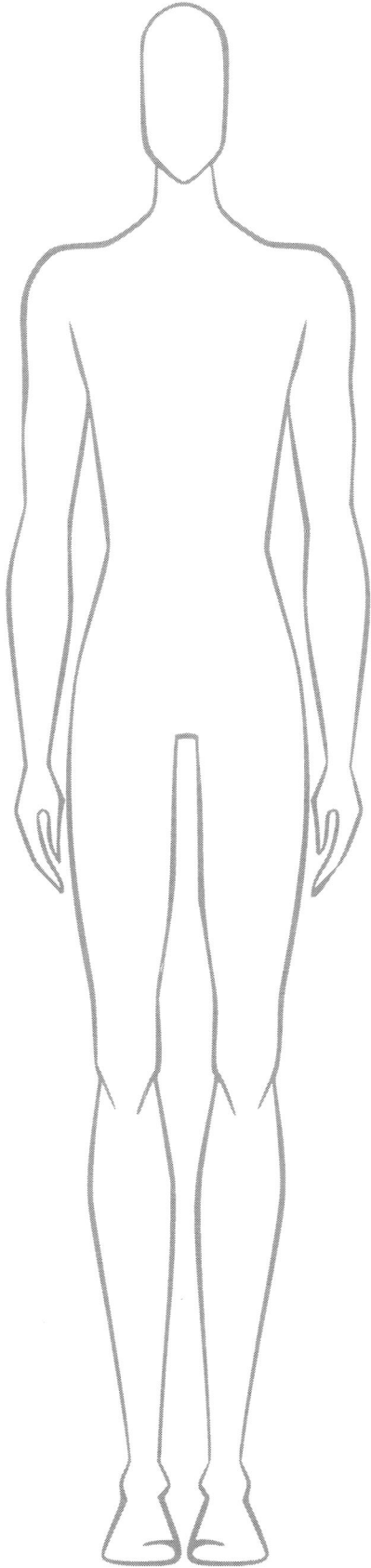

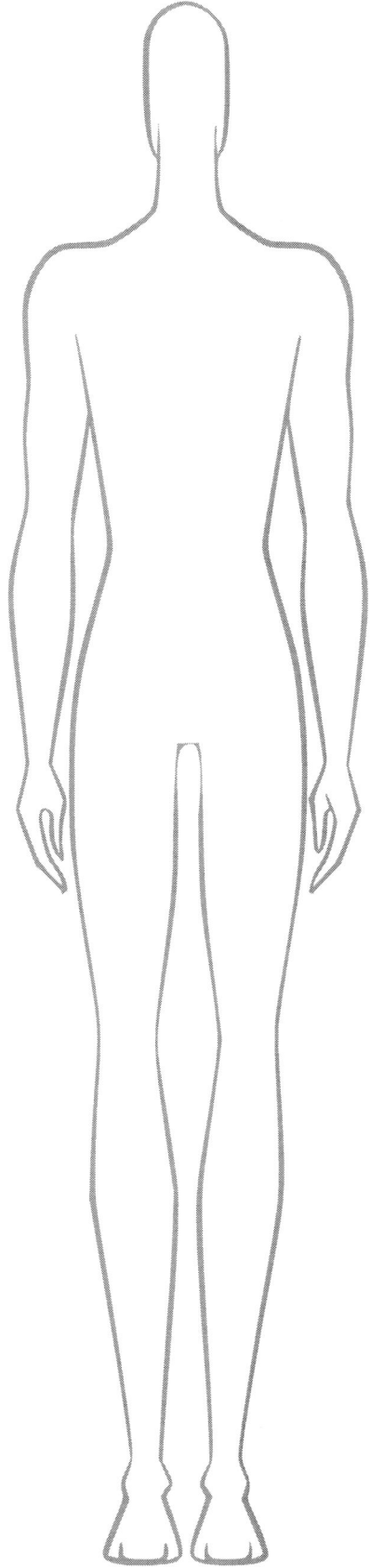

NOTES

Made in the USA
Las Vegas, NV
25 January 2022

42306660R00061